HAWKER HUNTER

M.J. Hardy

Foulis

Haynes

ISBN 0 85429 448 1

A **FOULIS** Aircraft Book

First published 1985

© **Winchmore Publishing Services Ltd 1985**

Published by:
Haynes Publishing Group
Sparkford,
Yeovil,
Somerset BA22 7JJ

Haynes Publications Inc.
861 Lawrence Drive,
Newbury Park,
California 91320, USA

Produced by:
Winchmore Publishing Services Limited,
40 Triton Square,
London NW1 3HG

Printed in England

British Library Cataloguing in Publication Data
Hardy, M.J.
Hawker Hunter super profile
1. Hunter (Turbo jet fighter planes)
I. Title
623.74'64 UG1242.F5
ISBN 0-85429-448-1.

Library of Congress Catalog
Card Number
84-48560

Avro Vulcan (F436)
B29 Superfortress (F339)
Grumman F8F Bearcat (F447)
Boeing 707 (F356)
de Havilland Mosquito (F422)
Douglas DC3 Dakota (F449)
Gloster Meteor (F451)
Harrier (F357)
Lockheed C130 Hercules (F450)
Mikoyan-Gurevich MiG 21 (F439)
P51 Mustang (F423)
Phantom II (F376)
Sea King (F377)
SEPECAT Jaguar (F438)

Contents

Super Etendard (F378)
Tiger Moth (F421)
Bell UH-1 Iroquois (F437)

Further titles in this series will be published at
regular intervals. For information on new titles
please contact your bookseller or write to the
publisher.

With the fine lines and good looks of a thoroughbred, the Hawker Hunter was undoubtedly Britain's most successful post-war fighter, as well as being delightful to fly. Its first flights in 1951 showed in no uncertain manner that this country had now broken away from the early doubts that had surrounded the swept wing in the immediate post-war years, and could now produce a transonic fighter of outstanding quality. Although the Hunter F.1 suffered badly from Avon engine surge when the guns were fired above a certain height, the Sapphire-engined Hunter F.2 and F.5 did not, although these latter variants were never built in large quantities. With the engine surge/gun firing problem and other earlier 'snags' behind it, the Hunter F.6 emerged as a formidable ground-attack aircraft that was, like the F.4, built under licence in Holland and Belgium and widely exported. However both development and production of this fine aircraft were cut short by the ill-judged 1957 Defence White Paper, with its vision of a future of push-button missile warfare, and the Hunter was never developed to fulfil its real technical and sales potential. Basically, this was the result of the loss of national self confidence and political will that

followed the Suez debacle of 1956. The projected fully supersonic thinner wing Hawker P.1083 development of the Hunter unfortunately never saw the light of day. Had development and production continued, Britain would have had a fighter and strike aircraft worthy to compete in world markets with US types such as the F–104 Starfighter, the Northrop F–5 series and the updated export variants of the McDonnell Douglas A–4 Skyhawk, and at least 500 – more probably 750 – more Hunters could have been built and sold. Even so, a flourishing trade in refurbished and updated Hunter F.6s for resale to foreign air forces developed, and some 300 fighters and 50 trainers went through this process to serve in new insignia in other lands.

Genesis

By 1944 the success of the jet engine in the Gloster E.28/39 and Meteor made it clear that this form of propulsion had passed through its early experimental stages and was no longer something untried and experimental, but the obvious

form of power plant for future fighters. At first Hawker's chief designer, Sydney Camm – later to be technical director and Sir Sydney – was not over-anxious to enter the field of jet propulsion, and he remained cool about the new aerodynamic data on swept wings emanating from Germany at the end of the war. This was ironical in view of the fact that his name was to be associated with the most successful British swept-wing fighter, the Hawker Hunter and, of course, the Harrier. The former had its genesis in Hawker's first jet fighter project, the P.1035 of November 1944, which was a redesign of the piston-engined F.2/43 Fury to take a Rolls-Royce RB.41 Nene turbojet in the forward fuselage, which exhausted through bifurcated jet pipes on each side of the cockpit. The MAP (Ministry of Aircraft Production) was unconvinced about the bifurcated jet pipe layout and so the P.1035 was discarded at the end of 1944 in favour of the P.1040, which was finally submitted in January 1946. This retained the bifurcated jet pipe

This late production Dutch-built Hunter F.6 N–274 belongs to No 325 Sqn based at Soesterberg, and has a carrier for a Sidewinder air-to-air missile on the outer wing pylon.

arrangement, and had intakes in the thickened roots of the mid wings for the 4,500-lb (2,041-kg) s.t. Nene 1 turbojet. RAF interest in the P.1040 lapsed but work proceeded on it for the Fleet Air Arm as a day interceptor to Specification N.7/46, and three prototypes were ordered on 28 May 1946.

Retaining the bifurcated jet pipe layout, which exhausted at the trailing edge of each wing root, offered several advantages. It made possible a much slimmer and less bulky fuselage than would have been the case if, like the P.1040's contemporary the Grumman F9F–2 Panther, the jet pipe was continued down the fuselage to exhaust under the tail, which made for a more complex tail structure. The bifurcated layout also makes possible an extra fuel tank in the rear fuselage, total fuel capacity being 395 Imp gals (1,796 litres) in four fuselage cells, and it also resulted in negligible thrust loss and no jet pipe overheating, as well as leaving much more of the fuselage internal space free of obstruction. The wing root intakes enabled the pilot to be placed well forward for the best possible view, and the four 20-mm Hispano Mk V cannon (with 200 rounds

per gun) to go in the lower fuselage underneath the cockpit floor; the forward-retracting nosewheel is mounted between and just ahead of them.

The P.1040 was among the sleekest and most elegant of the early post-war jet fighters, and the prototype, VP401, made its first flight in the hands of Squadron Leader T.S. 'Wimpey' Wade at Boscombe Down on 2 September 1947; it had no armament, wing folding mechanism or arrestor hook fitted, and no equipment except vhf radio. Early flights showed the need for a few minor modifications, such as the addition of 'pen nib' fairings at the wing roots aft of the jet nozzles, and VP401 went to the A&AEE at Boscombe Down for brief pre-view handling trials. A later Boscombe Down report praised the general handling and flying qualities, but considered air brakes to be vital for Service use, and criticised the lack of pressurisation and the manual flight control system. As the Malcolm pilot ejection system was found to be unsatisfactory, VP401's short test programme was not completed.

The second prototype, VP413, was the first fully 'navalised' Sea Hawk F.1, as the type was now

The Hawker P.1040 Sea Hawk introduced the wing root engine intakes later featured on the Hunter, and has bifurcated jet pipes at the trailing edge of the wing roots. WF144, seen here, is the second production Sea Hawk F.1.

known, and made its maiden flight on 3 September 1948. It had wings folding upwards hydraulically just outboard of the main under-carriage, a sting-type arrestor hook under the rudder, catapult points and armament fitted. Flight trials indicated the need for a 2-ft 6-in (76-cm) increase in wing span to 39 ft (11.89 m), which was duly incorporated, and the third prototype, VP422, which first flew on 17 October 1949, had provision for RATOG (Rocket Assisted Take-Off Gear), drop tanks and a faster retracting undercarriage. On 22 November 1949 an order for 151 Sea Hawks was placed, and Hawker built 35 F.1s before turning over complete responsibility for Sea Hawk production and development to Armstrong Whitworth in 1951 because of the super priority status now accorded to the Hunter as a result of the Korean war.

Production was to Specification 25/48P, which called for a 5,000-lb (2,270-kg) s.t. Nene 4 engine with cartridge starter, a

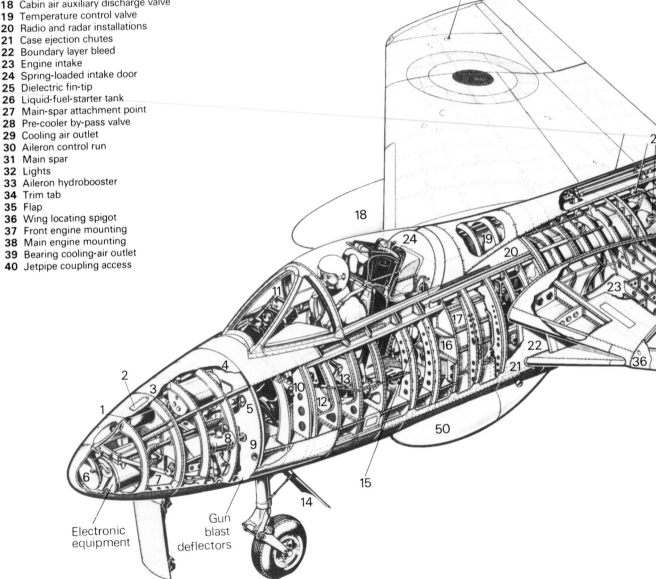

1 Battle camera
2 Camera magazine access
3 Oxygen bottles
4 Ram air valve
5 Cabin pressurization
6 Radar ranging
7 Ground pressurization connection
8 Anti-icing fluid tank
9 Forward pressurization bulkhead
10 Rudder pedals
11 Gun-sight
12 Control column
13 Engine controls
14 Forward-retracting nosewheel
15 Compressed air bottles (4)
16 Rear pressurization bulkhead
17 Gun pack
18 Cabin air auxiliary discharge valve
19 Temperature control valve
20 Radio and radar installations
21 Case ejection chutes
22 Boundary layer bleed
23 Engine intake
24 Spring-loaded intake door
25 Dielectric fin-tip
26 Liquid-fuel-starter tank
27 Main-spar attachment point
28 Pre-cooler by-pass valve
29 Cooling air outlet
30 Aileron control run
31 Main spar
32 Lights
33 Aileron hydrobooster
34 Trim tab
35 Flap
36 Wing locating spigot
37 Front engine mounting
38 Main engine mounting
39 Bearing cooling-air outlet
40 Jetpipe coupling access

41 Air-brake jack housing
42 Jetpipe rail
43 Rudder-level mounting
44 Hydraulic-accumulator
45 Tailplane actuator
46 Elevator booster
47 Rudder control-run
48 Trim-tab actuator
49 Tailplane pivot
50 100-gal (455l) plastic drop tanks

Electronic
equipment

Gun
blast
deflectors

This cutaway drawing of one of the
development Hunter F.6s, WW595, shows
the salient features of the type. Note the
control runs along the fuselage 'spine'.

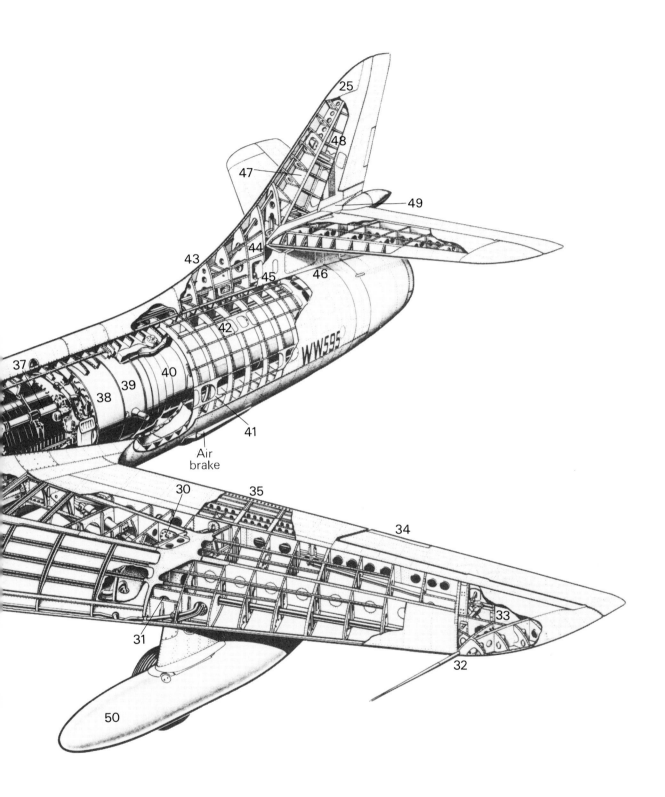

Air
brake

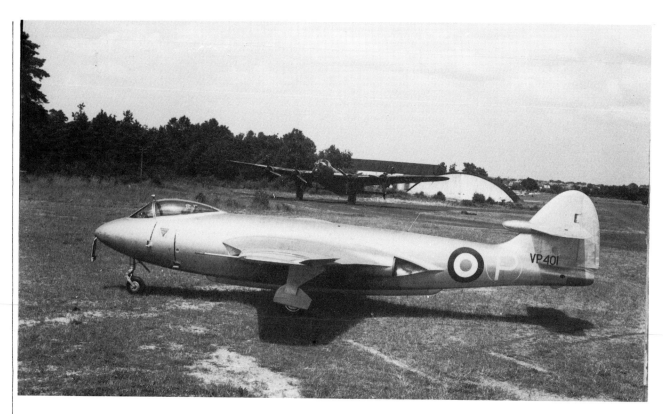

larger tailplane, air brakes, a pressurised cockpit with a Martin-Baker Mk 1D ejector seat, armour and shatter-proof windscreen, an undercarriage absorption capacity of 16 ft/second (4.88 m/sec) for deck landings, provision for rocket projectiles or bombs in place of drop tanks, and also provision for RATOG. Following deck landing trials on *HMS Eagle* by F.1s WF144 and WF145, the arrestor hook, which hung rather low, was modified to avoid giving trouble in service. Armstrong Whitworth built 60 Sea Hawk F.1s to add to the 35 built by Hawker, and these were followed by 40 Sea Hawk F.2s with powered ailerons, and 116 F.B.3s with underwing racks for two 500-lb (227-kg) bombs. After these came 90 FGA.4s with four underwing pylons for similar bombs, and then 86 FGA.6s with the more powerful Nene 103 turbojet of 5,400-lb (2,450-kg) s.t. in place of the Nene 101 of earlier marks. Many F.B.3s were converted to F.B.5s by fitting them with the Nene 103 engine, and many FGA.4s were similarly

modified up to FGA.6 standard. The Sea Hawk F.1 first entered service with No 806 Squadron in March 1953, and altogether Sea Hawks equipped 19 FAA squadrons.

During 1956-57 22 Sea Hawk FGA.50s, an export variant of the FGA.6, were supplied to the Dutch Naval Air Arm for use on the carrier *Karel Doorman*. They equipped No 860 Squadron and were later modified to carry two Sidewinder missiles; when Grumman Trackers embarked on their parent ship in 1960 they moved to a shore base at Valkenburg, where some also equipped No 3 Squadron together with Meteor T.7s. The West German Kriegsmarine, or Naval Air Arm, took delivery of 34 Sea Hawk Mk 100 fighter bombers similar to the FGA.6 for use from shore bases. These differed from previous marks in having a taller fin and rudder, a revised cockpit layout, American radio and provision for four drop tanks on underwing pylons. These were followed by another 34 Sea Hawk

The Hawker P.1040 prototype VP401 is seen here as the P.1072 with an Armstrong Siddeley Assn.1 Snarler rocket engine in the extreme tail. Note the fairing under the fuselage for the rocket fuel lines.

Mk 101 reconnaissance fighter variants for the Kriegsmarine with Ecko Type 34 radar in a pod under the starboard wing; the Mk 100 could carry two 500-lb (227-kg) bombs and two drop tanks, or 20 3-in (76-mm) or 16 5-in (127-mm) rocket projectiles under the wings. The German Sea Hawks retained their arrestor hooks and other shipboard equipment even though they operated only from land bases. Three years after production had ceased, the Indian Navy ordered 24 Sea Hawk FGA.6s, half new and half ex-Royal Navy aircraft, and these equipped two squadrons on India's aircraft carrier *Vikrant*. Eventually the Indians bought 74 Sea Hawks, which served afloat and ashore until 1977, by which time they were the last of the type in service anywhere.

Meanwhile at the end of the war much more detailed knowledge

became available on the rocket-powered Messerschmitt Me 163 Komet interceptor, and in October 1945 Hawker became interested in the rocket motor as a means of boosting speed. But this interest waned in view of the absence at that time of any suitable British rocket engine, although it revived when the Armstrong Siddeley ASSn.1 Snarler rocket motor became available. This engine, which gave a maximum of 2,000-lb (910-kg) s.t. at sea level, was fitted in the rear fuselage of the P.1040 prototype VP401, which thus modified became the P.1072; the same Nene 4 turbojet as before provided the main power, and the P.1072 first flew with the Snarler from the Armstrong Siddeley airfield at Bitteswell on 20 November 1950. The Snarler could be switched on and off by the pilot, and used a mixture of liquid oxygen and water methanol as fuel, enough being carried for 2.75 minutes firing at full thrust. The Snarler's fuel lines were carried in a long skid-like fairing under the fuselage, and the

rocket motor's weight (without fuel) was only 215 lb (98 kg). Some half a dozen test flights were made with the P.1072 using the Snarler's thrust, but further test flying ceased after the Air Ministry decided to back reheat rather than the rocket motor as a means of increasing thrust.

While there was still official interest in the rocket motor Hawker had proposed two developments of the P.1040, the P.1046 for the Royal Navy and the P.1047, both with tail-mounted rocket engines.

The P.1047 project had swept wings, and this led to the P.1052 to Specification E.38/46, originally developed as a research aircraft to provide data on the characteristics of swept wings, especially their controllability and stability at low speeds. It featured a wing sweepback of 35° on the quarter-chord line with a Hawker H10% symmetrical wing section, and an aspect ratio of 3.84, and was powered by a 5,000-lb (2,270-kg) s.t. RN.2 Nene 4; in fact, it retained the same fuselage,

The first major step towards the Hunter was the Hawker P.1052, built to investigate swept-wing characteristics. Seen here is the first P.1052, VX272.

unswept tail unit, landing gear and engine as the Sea Hawk, with only slight modifications to the wing root intakes, and unlike some other swept-wing types, the P.1052 was not fitted with leading edge slots for safe lateral control at the stall.

The P.1052 prototype VX272 made its first flight at Boscombe Down on 19 November 1948 in the hands of 'Wimpey' Wade, and was followed into the air by a second prototype, VX279, on 13 April 1949. This underwent pre-view handling and performance trials at Boscombe Down in July 1949 to determine its suitability as an interceptor fighter. To this end it was flown in mock combat with a Meteor F.4 between 12,000 ft (3,658 m) and 25,000 ft (7,620 m), but the P.1052's elevator control was found to be too heavy for a fighter, lacking in effectiveness and with poor response, which proved to be very tiring for the pilot. But apart from this the P.1052 was pleasant to fly, and the ailerons were delightfully quick throughout the speed range, the rate of roll being good. The swept wings gave a usable Mach number of 0.9 but also introduced the problem of Dutch roll.

On 13 May 1949 VX272 flew from London to Paris in unfavourable weather conditions, covering the 212 miles (341 km) distance in 21 minutes 27.8 seconds at an average speed of 618.27 mph (994.8 km/h). In July that year a preliminary deck landing assessment of VX279 was made under ADDL (Aerodrome Dummy Deck Landing) conditions, and this showed that it was a very nice aircraft in which to make ADDLs and that it had better slow speed handling qualities than the P.1040. VX272 was later fitted with a deck arrestor hook and flew at the 1951 SBAC Display in the current Royal Navy fighter markings. Earlier it had been fitted with the mock-up of an auxiliary rocket motor known as the Beta under the tail, but this was removed.

The P.1052 clearly had the makings of a very promising fighter and, having so much commonality with the Sea Hawk, it could have gone into production very quickly. The Australian Government was sufficiently interested to want to build a version of the P.1052 powered by the Rolls-Royce Tay with reheat under licence at the Commonwealth Aircraft Corporation plant at Fishermen's Bend near Melbourne for the Royal Australian Air Force. Final agreements to do this were signed with the Hawker Siddeley Group in March 1950 following Hawker's proposal in January for a reheat Tay-engined P.1052. Because the bifurcated jet pipe arrangement of the P.1040 and P.1052 would not have been suitable for a reheat installation, the P.1052 was redesigned into the P.1081 with a more conventional 'straight

through' jet pipe exhausting under the rudder, and both the fin and the tailplane were now swept back, with the tailplane mounted nearly midway up the fin. Because the future of the Tay remained unsettled, the P.1081 was designed around the 5,000-lb (2,270-kg) s.t. RN.2 Nene 4 as fitted in the P.1052 and the

P.1081 prototype was in fact the second P.1052, VX279, modified to have the redesigned rear fuselage and tail, the wing and forward fuselage being the same as the P.1052's, with the same wing span of 31 ft 6 in (9.6 m). As the P.1081, VX279 was first flown by 'Wimpey' Wade on 19 June 1950 and it eventually

the Tay 250 and in a more powerful derivative known as the Verdon. Advanced developments of the Tay gave up to 8,750 lb (3,969 kg) s.t. and served, in the US Navy's Grumman F9F-8T (later TF-9J) Cougar trainer until the early 1970s.

These engines were both cheaper and generally more powerful and effective than contemporary axial-flow turbojets such as the General Electric J47 and the first production Rolls-Royce Avons, which started at 6,500 lb (2,950 kg) s.t. Since this thrust was about the same as the Tay would have achieved, no doubt it seemed sensible at the time to curtail the Tay's development in favour of the Avon family. It was a decision that was to cost the British aircraft industry dearly for, deprived of the Tay-powered P.1081 in the absence of an RAF order, the Australians turned elsewhere for their fighter requirements and, in October 1951, acquired a licence from North American to build the F-86E Sabre at the Commonwealth Aircraft Corporation plant, this being re-engined with the Avon for Australian requirements. A Tay-powered P.1081 would have had obvious export possibilities and might well, like the Meteor and Hunter, have been built in Holland and Belgium and perhaps other countries as well. Various modifications were made to the P.1081 prototype in the five months after its first flight as the result of test flying and, with the ending of Australian interest in the type, it was transferred to the RAE. On 3 April 1951 it crashed, killing the pilot, 'Wimpey' Wade, and the cause of the accident was unknown.

achieved Mach 0.89 at 36,000 ft (10,973 m).

Sadly, in spite of the Australian interest, the Air Staff refused to back either the P.1052 or the P.1081 with an RAF order, nor was Sydney Camm able to persuade them to buy the reheat Tay-engined P.1081 which the Australians wanted, because it was felt that the centrifugal flow Nene and Tay would soon give way to and be made obsolete by axial-flow engines such as the new Rolls-Royce Avon. So in the end the Tay never went into large-scale production in Britain, although it was built under licence by Pratt & Whitney as the J48 and by Hispano-Suiza in France both as

The Hunter Emerges

Although the P.1052 and P.1081 did not go into production through lack of a home market, a separate line of Hawker development ensured that their successor, the Hunter, would follow on naturally. Hawker had considered projects both to Specification F.43/46 for a day interceptor to replace the Meteor, and to F.44/46 for a two-seat day and night fighter; these were to have had alternative armaments of either four 30-mm Aden cannon or a single big 4.5-in (114.3-mm) recoilless gun firing a clip of 6-10 big rounds. Gloster also considered projects to these requirements, and they eventually resulted in the GA.5 Javelin, while in October 1947 Hawker proposed the P.1067 project, which almost met the needs of Spec F.43/46. Sydney Camm felt that neither this nor the F.44/46 requirement would result in a good aeroplane, so the P.1067 was continued as a private venture, with a Rolls-Royce AJ.65 or Avon or a Metrovick F.9 (later to become the Armstrong Siddeley Sapphire) axial-flow turbojet. A plain nose intake was featured, and a T-tail to avoid pitch-up at high subsonic speeds, and armament was two 30-mm Aden guns in the fuselage. In January 1948 the P.1067 project was submitted and accepted, and Specification F.3/48 was written around it in March that year.

The need for a radar ranging gun sight in the nose with its scanner led to the air intakes being repositioned in the wing roots; they were basically similar to the Sea Hawk's, and made the wing roots deep enough for strong spars with booms of steel, as well as for housing the main wheels in the centre section outside the fuselage. Wing sweep was finally 40° at the quarter chord line, with a thickness/chord ratio of 8.5 per cent and an aspect ratio of 3.3. The main flaps, like those of the P.1052 and P.1081, were stressed to act as air brakes – which was to be a source of trouble later on – and the tailplane was now lowered to just over half way down the fin. The four 30-mm Aden guns, which had 150 rounds per gun, were, with their breeches and magazines, in a single package which could be lowered in and out of the lower fuselage as a unit by a winch, or replaced by another similar unit, leaving the cannon barrels in place under the cockpit floor. This detachable gun pack, together with single-point pressure refuelling through the port main wheel bay, made turn-round times between sorties of as little as 7 minutes possible. The fuselage was built in three main sections, the nose containing the cockpit, armament pack and nosewheel, the centre section with integral wing roots, intake ducts and engine mountings, and the detachable rear fuselage with integral fin base and removable jet pipe and tail cone. The main wheels retracted inwards and the nosewheel forwards, and in emergency they could be lowered pneumatically. Internal fuel capacity of the Hunter F.1 and F.2 was 334 Imp gals (1,518 litres) and these marks had no provision for external 'stores' or drop tanks.

In June 1948 three P.1067 prototypes, WB188 and WB195 with Avons and WB202 with the Armstrong Siddeley Sapphire, were ordered. The Avon was always intended to be the main engine, because of the Rolls-Royce reputation, and this view did not change when the gun firing troubles due to engine surge later occurred. Metropolitan Vickers or Metrovick had run the first F.9 turbojet in May 1948, and when this firm decided to leave the aero engine field the F.9's development was taken over by Armstrong Siddeley Motors Ltd that October; they considerably redesigned it in the process, and the F.9 became the Sapphire. Work on the P.1067 prototypes proceeded fairly slowly for a time, but with the outbreak of the Korean War in June 1950 a dramatic new impetus was given to the programme, and work on the prototypes was speeded up on a three-shift basis. In October 1950 200 Avon-powered P.1067s were ordered from Hawker, and Armstrong Whitworth received an order for 200 Sapphire-powered ones, while an additional 151 were also ordered from Gloster Aircraft Co Ltd, but this order was later cancelled as the firm was unable to handle it.

Fears of a new confrontation with Russia or China led a 'super priority' status to be accorded to the P.1067 and several other new British combat aircraft, and gearing up to large-scale production of the type went ahead with almost wartime urgency. Europe was scoured for 3,250 machine tools, and over 40,000 jigs and fixtures, over 11,000 of the latter finally being acquired on the continent, as well as more than 1,800 specialist machine tools. As well as the Hawker plant at Kingston and Armstrong Whitworth's factory at Baginton, the big Squires Gate shadow factory in which Vickers Wellington bombers had been built during the war was reactivated and retooled to meet the need for P.1067s, being run by Hawker Aircraft (Blackpool) Ltd, and plans were well advanced before the prototype flew for no less than 14 assembly lines at these three plants. Avon production was also widely subcontracted, these engines being built by D. Napier & Son, the Standard Motor Co and Bristol's Engine Division at Filton, as well as by Rolls-Royce.

The prototype WB188, painted duck egg green, made its maiden flight on 20 July 1951 at Boscome Down in the hands of chief test pilot Neville Duke; during a fast taxi run earlier on he had burnt out the brakes. The first flight of 47 minutes was successful, but because of an

Right: The duck egg-green Hawker P.1067 prototype WB188 on the runway at Farnborough during the 1951 SBAC Display; note the large flap area. Neville Duke was at that time the only British test pilot to wear the USAF-type 'bone dome' pilot's helmet.

Below: The Hawker P.1067 mock-up seen here originally featured a T-tail to avoid pitch-up at high subsonic speeds. The tailplane was later lowered to midway down the fin.

The second prototype P.1067 WB195, seen here, had the removable 30-mm Aden gun pack fitted, and a radar-ranging gun sight. Note the tear drop-shaped fairing at the rudder/elevator junction, fitted to cure severe tail buffeting encountered near Mach 1.

The third prototype WB202, which was Hawker-built, and powered by the 8,000-lb (3,629-kg) s.t. ASSa.6 Sapphire 101 turbojet, first flew at Dunsfold on 30 November 1952 and featured an increase in length of 7.5 in (19.05 cm) which was later made standard for all Hunters. The Sapphire-powered Hunter F.2 was in fact marginally faster than the Avon-powered F.1, yet only 150 of the Sapphire-engined F.2s and F.5s were built.

The first prototype WB188 was later modified up to Hunter F.3 standard with 'petal'-type air brakes on the rear fuselage, an RA.7R Avon with afterburning giving 9,600 lb (4,355 kg) s.t. with reheat, and a nose and windscreen modified to reduce drag. In this form WB188 flown by Neville Duke set up a world absolute air speed record of 727.6 mph (1,171 km/h) on 7 September 1953 over the 3-km straight course between Littlehampton and West Worthing off the Sussex coast that had been used for the 1946 speed record attempt with Meteor F.IVs. This was followed by a 100-km (62.1-miles) closed circuit course speed record of 709 mph (1,136 km/h) set up in bad weather. Such was the pace of fighter development at this time that Duke's speed record was broken twice within a month, first by Lieutenant Commander M.J. Lithgow in the Supermarine Swift F.4 at 737.3 mph (1,186 km/h) at Castel Idris in Libya, and then, on 3 October at Muroc in California, by the Douglas XF4D-1 Skyray prototype flown by Lieutenant Commander James Verdin, US Navy, who achieved 752.9 mph (1,211.746 km/h). This aircraft, flown by test pilot R. Rahn, broke the 100-km closed

earlier decision to disconnect the hydraulic boost the elevator forces were large, and there was a lack of tailplane trim on landing, while the powered ailerons proved to be very sensitive. With the elevator boost connected WB188 was soon exceeding 700 mph (1,126.5 km/h) at low levels, but at height severe tail buffeting was encountered at indicated airspeeds near Mach 1. This trouble was finally cured by fitting a tear-drop shaped fairing at the junction of the rudder and elevators. Before this fairing provided the cure a variety of other modifications were tried, such as fitting spoilers on the fin, turbulators on the fin and tail, a shortened rudder, an additional dorsal fin, and modifying the rear end shape around the jet pipe area. But it was not until 6 June 1952 that the fairing at the rudder/ elevator junction enabled the first vibration-free flight at high indicated Mach number to be made. Before the P.1067's first flight, Neville Duke had flown the experimental Fairey Firefly 4 fitted with powered controls similar to those of the P.1067, as well as a Sea Fury fitted with a powered elevator system; these served as

test beds for the then largely untried concept of powered controls.

The first prototype did not have armament fitted and was powered by a 7,500-lb (3,175-kg) s.t. RA.7 Avon, the shattering roar of which thrilled the crowds at the 1951 Farnborough show when Duke made some very low-level passes at about 700 mph (1,126 km/h). By June 1952 WB188 was making sonic booms fairly frequently, and US elevation of the type led to some major Off-Shore Procurement orders for the Hunter, as it was now known.

The second prototype WB195 first flew on 5 May 1952, and had the removable 30 mm Aden gun pack fitted, as well as a radar ranging Mk 5 (later Mk 8) gun sight, two 10-channel vhf radios and the Rebecca/Eureka and DME navaids; it was powered by the fully-developed RA.7 Avon 104. At Farnborough in 1952 Duke gave the assembled crowds what was for most of them their first experience of a sonic boom, when he exceeded Mach 1 in a dive started at 43,000 ft (13,106 m) over Dunsfold, the boom being aimed to arrive over Farnborough.

circuit record a fortnight later. It was at high temperatures that sound travelled fastest, so warm climates like Libya or California rather than Britain were best for record attempts by transonic fighters, as higher speeds could be achieved without going through the sound barrier. Duke's record speed was Mach 0.944 at a temperature of 74°F, Lithgow in the Swift achieved Mach 0.926 in a temperature of 102°F in his attempt, and Commander Verdin in the XF4D-1 achieved Mach 0.964 at 98.5°F, so if Duke had enjoyed the warmer conditions of Libya his record would probably have lasted longer. The Hunter F.3 variant did not go into production.

Above: WB188 modified to Hunter F.3 standard and finished red all over for the 1953 world speed record attempt. Just visible under the white serial is the hinge fairing for the 'petal'-type fuselage air brake, and the nose is now sharply pointed and the windscreen modified.

Top: The Korean war gave a considerable impetus to Hunter production. Hunter F.4s are seen here in final assembly at Kingston.

Squadron Service and Early Snags

The first production Hunter F.1, WT555, made its first flight on 16 May 1953 and its serial number caused it to be named 'State Express' after the State Express 555 cigarette, a popular brand of the 1950s. The first Sapphire-powered Hunter F.2, WN888, made its maiden flight five months later, on 14 October. Altogether 113 Hunter F.1s were built at Kingston and 26 more (commencing WW599) at Squires Gate, and three of the early production aircraft, WT555, WT573 and WT576 went to the Aeroplane & Armament Experimental Establishment at Boscombe Down for the type's C(A) release evalutations from November 1953 to June 1954. Development of the Hunter had been smooth and entry into service would have been rapid but for two unrelated problems which together delayed entry into squadron service by months and seriously affected the type's operational effectiveness. It was not until May 1954 that the first Hunter F.1s reached the Central Fighter Establishment at West Raynham, Norfolk, and not until July that year that the first Hunter F.1 squadron, No. 43 at RAF Leuchars in Scotland, was formed, giving up its Meteor F.8s for the new jets.

The two problems which gave so much trouble were the use of the Hunter's main landing flaps as air brakes, and the Avon's susceptibility to surging, or the sudden violently unstable breakdown of air flow through the compressor. This meant that the guns could not be fired above about 10,000 ft (3,048 m) under practically all conditions as the resulting surge could damage the engine and might also result in a flameout. The Hunter's main flaps had small perforations in them and, like those of the P.1052 and P.1081, had been designed and stressed for use as air brakes and to remain fully open at speeds up to 620 knots (714 mph). When the flaps were lowered at high speed there was considerable trim change, and this was intended to be corrected by small 'dive recovery' flaps on the underside of the wing at the 25 per cent chord line. These failed to give the required nose-up pitching moment, and an urgent search for a solution got under way. This led first to divided flaps being tried, with only the inboard 40 per cent each side being used as air brakes, but extending these persistently caused a pitch change that was felt to be unacceptable for air combat. Another solution tried on the prototype WB188 in its Hunter F.3 form was 'petal'-type air brakes on the rear fuselage.

Had the problem been diagnosed earlier this type might have been adopted, but with large-scale production deliveries of the Hunter building up, a rather hasty improvisation in the shape of a single air brake under the rear fuselage was finally adopted; this was hinged at its forward end to extend downward through 67°, and was not even recessed to be flush with the fuselage underside. Of the three Hunter F.1s at Boscombe Down, WT555 could not be fitted with the under-fuselage air brake, but this was fitted to WT573 and WT576, and different styles of the brake were tried out. WT555 later had a tail braking parachute fitted, but did not fly with this until mid-May 1954 due to some difficulties with its design and installation. As a result of testing the air brake at Boscombe Down, an increase in its drag was among the desirable improvements recommended for production aircraft.

When Rolls-Royce started design of the AJ.65 or Avon not long after the war, not a great deal was known about axial-flow compressors, at least in this country, and even Rolls, with their great experience, needed about four years to get the first production version right; this was the 6,500-lb (2,950-kg) s.t. RA.3 Avon 103 for the Canberra. The Avon compressor suffered badly from surging, and the remedy adopted was the addition of triple blow-off valves on the compressor casing and variable-swirl inlet guide vanes driven by a pneumatic ram that was responsive to compressor speed. This problem occurred with the RA.7 Avon 104 that was first fitted to the second prototype WB195, and persisted with the RA.7 Avon 107 variant with hot air intake anti-icing. This was still not finally cured on the

Left: This view of Hunter FGA.9 XK151 shows the under-fuselage air brake fully extended through 67°.

Right: The first production Hunter F.1 WT555 was named 'State Express', after the State Express 555 cigarette. It was not fitted with the under-fuselage air brake, but later featured a tail-braking parachute for shortening the landing run.

7,600-lb (3,447-kg) s.t. RA.21 Avon 113 with increased nozzle guide vane area, the Mk 113 being the variant stipulated as the standard Hunter F.1 engine as a result of Boscombe Down C(A) release trials. The surge problem was finally eliminated by fuel dipping, or briefly reducing the fuel flow as the guns were fired. Of the three aircraft on these trials, WT555 first had an Avon 104 and later changed to a Mk 113, while WT573 and WT576 had Avon 107s. Most of the early gun-firing trials had been done with the Sapphire-engined Hunter F.2 prototype, and this engine was free from the surge problem; the F.2 was cleared to fire high-velocity ammunition up to 48,000 ft (14,440 m) and 550 knots (632.5 mph) while the Avon-powered F.1 was cleared to fire its guns only to 25,000 ft (7,625 m) and 250 knots (287.5 mph). Yet in spite of this disadvantage, there was no switch-over of Hunter contracts from the F.1 to the Sapphire-powered F.2.

The Boscombe Down assessment praised the Hunter's flying qualities and its cockpit layout, comfort and visibility, but recommended several points of future improvement, such as the early introduction of Dunlop Maxaret anti-skid wheel brakes, and a reduction in the heaviness of the elevator control at high IAS and Indicated Mach Number. This resulted in new fully powered elevators with different linkage and spring feel and later, in 1957, a 'flying tail' was introduced on the Hunter F.6 production lines in which the power-operated elevator was interconnected to change the tailplane incidence electrically. The Fairey-powered flight-control system was very sensitive, but over a period the flight controls were greatly improved. Fully-powered ailerons plus spring feel were introduced from 1954 because of criticisms of aileron forces necessary at high IAS, the aileron gear ratio in the manual mode was changed, and false aileron locks that entirely eliminated manual control were later deleted.

As many as 20 of the 139 Hunter F.1s built were used for pre-squadron service test flying, especially on the engine surge/gun-firing problem. The Hunter had a fully automatic Martin-Baker Mk 2H ejector seat, and it was not long before this was used successfully at supersonic speed by an RAF pilot who ejected safely after control difficulties at an Indicated Mach Number of between 1.01 and 1.1 at 25,000 ft (7,620 m), or about 725 mph (1,167 km/h) True Air Speed. The pilot's only major injury was a broken arm due to slipstream effect, as he had actuated and pulled the face blind with one hand. Minimum height for safe ejection with the Mk 2H seat was at first 400 ft (121.9 m) but after being fitted with the Duplex drogue this seat could be used down to 125 ft (38.1 m). The advantages of this lower safety height were felt to be sufficiently great for all existing Martin-Baker seats in service to be fitted retrospectively with the Duplex drogue system, priority being given to the RAF's Hunters with their Mk 2H seats, which were retrofitted in record time. Hunters of the 2nd Tactical Air Force were modified from 1955 on a 'fly-in' basis at Lyneham by Service working parties, while Martin-Baker technicians supervised the retrofitting at Fighter Command Hunter bases. Later the Mk 2H seats in Hunters were brought up to the standard of the Mk 3 seat with a higher rejection velocity from the aircraft, while another closely related improvement was the retrofitting to Hunters of power cockpit-hood jettisoning actuated by the seat's face blind.

The RAF's first operational Hunter F.1 squadron was No 43, which took delivery of its first F.1s at Leuchars in Fifeshire in July 1954, these replacing its Meteor F.8s. The squadron had flown aircraft by the Hawker Siddeley Group and its predecessors since starting in 1916 with Sopwith 1½-

Hunter F.1 WT656, seen here, was fitted experimentally with blown flaps.

Strutters, these being followed by
Sopwith Camels and Snipes. These
were followed by Gloster
Gamecock 1s, Armstrong
Whitworth Siskin IIIAs, Hawker
Fury 1s and Hurricanes in the
inter-war years from 1926, and
the squadron badge featured a
game cock to commemorate its
association with this Gloster type.
A break with the Hawker Siddeley
tradition occurred when Spitfires
were flown during 1943-47, but
Meteor F.4s and F.8s equipped
No 43 in the early post-war years.
The Hunter F.1s stayed until
August 1956, being replaced by
Hunter F.4s during March to
December 1956 and by F.6s from
the beginning of 1957. The
second Hunter unit was No 222
Squadron, also Leuchars-based,
receiving its first F.1s in December
1954 to replace its Meteor F.8s;
the F.1s were replaced in August
1956 by Hunter F.4s which
served until the squadron was
disbanded on 1 November 1957.
It was reformed in May 1960 as a
Bloodhound surface-to-air missile
unit at Woodhall Spa in
Lincolnshire. No 54 Squadron at
Odiham, Hampshire, was the third
to receive Hunter F.1s in March
1955 to replace their Meteor F.8s;
the F.1s were flown for only six
months before being replaced by
Hunter F.4s in September 1955,
which were themselves succeeded
by F.6s in January 1957. A fourth
squadron, No 247, also at Odiham,
started to re-equip with Hunter
F.1s in June 1955 but after only a
month these were replaced by
F.4s. F.1s also equipped Nos 229
and 233 Operational Conversion
Units.

Two non-standard Hunter F.1s
were WT656, which was modified
to have blown flaps, and WT571,
which had an area-ruled fuselage.

The Sapphire Hunters
Although the Armstrong Siddeley
Sapphire turbojet in the Hunter F.2
was free from the troublesome
engine-surge problem and its
effect on firing the guns that
plagued the Avon-engined F.1,

Hunters with the former engine
were never built in large numbers;
in fact only 150 of the Sapphire-
engined Hunter F.2s and F.5s
were built, which was 50 less than
the original order for 200
Sapphire-engined Hunters placed
in October 1950. There was no
change over of contracts from
Avon-engined F.1s to F.2s when
the Avon's surge problems were at
their height, partly because the
Rolls-Royce engine was also
committed to large-scale
production by Napier, Bristol and
Standard Motors, but also because
the Avon was always regarded as
the main Hunter engine, and the
Sapphire more as an insurance
policy. So even though Armstrong
Siddeley Motors Ltd, its makers,
were a Hawker Siddeley Group
company, and the Sapphire-
engined Hunter would have had
the Group's sales organisation
behind it in winning any export
orders, in fact no Sapphire-engined
Hunters were sold abroad. The
Hawker-built third prototype
Hunter WB202, which was the
first F.2 and was powered by an
8,000-lb (3,629-kg) s.t. ASSa.6

Hunter F.1s WW645:S, WT618:O,
WT622:G and WT582:D of No 43 Sqn,
the first to be equipped with the type. The
squadron checkerboard markings each side
of the roundel are black and white.

Sapphire 101, first flew at
Dunsfold on 30 November 1952,
and featured the 7.5-in
(19.05-cm) increase in length that
later became standard for all
Hunters. Most of the early gun-
firing trials were done with this
aircraft, which resulted in the F.2
being cleared to fire its guns at
much higher speeds and altitudes
than the Avon-engined F.1, as
previously mentioned.

The first production Hunter F.2,
WN888, made its maiden flight on
14 October 1953 and 45 of this
mark were built by Armstrong
Whitworth at Baginton. Like the
F.1, the F.2 was basically a short-
range day interceptor with no
provision for drop tanks or other
external 'stores'. With slightly more
thrust, the F.2 was marginally
faster than the F.1, and could
attain 698 mph (1,123 km/h or
Mach 0.905) at sea level, and 620
mph (998.4 km/h or Mach 0.94)
at 36,000 ft (10,950 m), while

the F.1 with Avon 113 could achieve 693 mph (1,114.7 km/h or Mach 0.9) at sea level and 617 mph (993.5 km/h or Mach 0.935) at 36,000 ft (10.950 m). Hunter F.2s equipped two squadrons, Nos 257 and 263, both based at Wattisham in Suffolk. No 257 was the first to receive its F.2s in September 1954, these replacing Meteor F.8s and being supplemented by Sapphire-engined Hunter F.5s from July 1955. Both these marks were flown together until the squadron was disbanded on 29 March 1957. No 263's Hunter F.2s began replacing their Meteor F.8s in February 1955 and were joined by some F.5s in April that year; like No 257, both these marks were operated together until October 1957, when both variants were replaced by the Hunter F.6, No 263 being redesignated No 1 Squadron on 1 July 1958.

The Hunter F.5 had the same Sapphire 101 engine as the F.2 but differed from it in having the same increased internal fuel capacity in additional leading edge fuel cells as the Hunter F.4, which increased the total internal fuel from 334 to 414 Imp gals (1,518 to 1,882 litres). The F.5, like the F.4, also had two underwing pylons on each of which could be carried a 100-Imp gal (454-litres) Bristol drop tank of asbestos phenolic plastic. The first production Hunter F.5, WN954, made its first flight on 19 October 1954 and 105 were built by Armstrong Whitworth, following the F.2 in production. In addition to Nos 257 and 263 Squadrons already mentioned, Hunter F.5s equipped Nos 1, 34, 41, 56 and 208 Squadrons.

No 56 at Waterbeach in Cambridgeshire was the first to re-equip with F.5s, which arrived in May 1955 to replace the Supermarine Swift F1s and F.2s which had had to be withdrawn as unsuitable, No 56 having been the first to equip with the Swift (the RAF's first swept-wing fighter) in February 1954. The Hunter F.5s

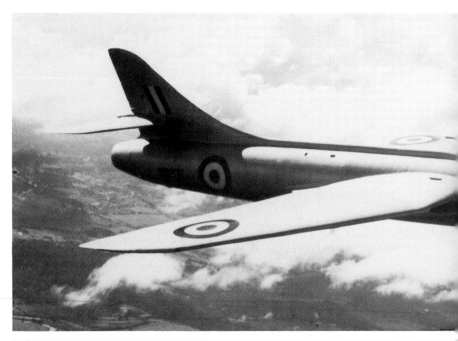

Left: The third prototype Hunter WB202, seen here, was the first F.2, with an Armstrong Siddeley ASSa.6 Sapphire 101 engine. It featured a 7.5-in (19.05-cm) increase in length that became standard for all Hunters, but the F.2 was otherwise externally identical to the F.1.

Below Left: Hunter F.5 WN958 with twelve 3-in rocket projectiles in three tiers of four under each wing tip, and two 100-Imp gal (454-litre) drop tanks.

Bottom Left: Hunter F.4 WT703 with twelve 3-in rocket projectiles and a 100-Imp gal (454-litre) drop tank under the port wing.

Below: Hunter F.4 XF310 was used for trials of the Fairey Fireflash beam-riding air-to-air missile. Ecko radar was fitted in the longer and more pointed nose. XF310 was later converted into a T.7 and was still serving with No 2 TWU in 1980.

Bottom: Hunter F.4 ID44 or 044 of the Belgian Air Force, seen in the Musée de l'Armée et d'Histoire Militaire in Brussels.

served until November 1958 when they were replaced by F.6s, which in turn gave way to the first Lightnings in January 1961. Next unit with the F.5s was No 41 Squadron at Biggin Hill, which flew them from August 1955 until the squadron disbanded on 31 January 1958, while No 1 Squadron at Tangmere, West Sussex, flew F.5s from September 1955 to 23 June 1958 when it too was disbanded, to be succeeded eight days later by the renumbered 263 Squadron which became the new No 1 Squadron and flew Hunter F.6s from Stradishall in Suffolk. No 34 Squadron, also based at Tangmere, flew F.5s from February 1956 to its disbandment on 10 January 1958 and during the Suez campaign of October 1956 both No 1 and 34 Squadron Hunter F.5s operated from Nicosia in Cyprus, flying defensive patrols over the island. When No 34 Squadron disbanded in January 1958, its Hunter F.5s were taken over at Tangmere by the air echelon of No 208 Squadron, who flew them to Nicosia in Cyprus in March that year; they were soon replaced by F.6s which were used until No 208 was disbanded on 30 March 1959.

The full potentialities of the Sapphire-engined Hunter, both technically and commercially in export sales, were never really fulfilled by the limited production of F.2s and F.5s. No mark of Hunter was produced with the more powerful 200-series Sapphires, with thrusts in the five-figure bracket, although one was used as a test bed for the 8,500-lb (3,856-kg) s.t. ASSa.12 Sapphire.

Development and First Export Orders

The Hunter was a fine aeroplane but one of the main shortcomings of the first two marks was a very limited operational radius of action; the F.1 and F.2 had no provision for drop tanks or other external 'stores'. So the first step in Hunter

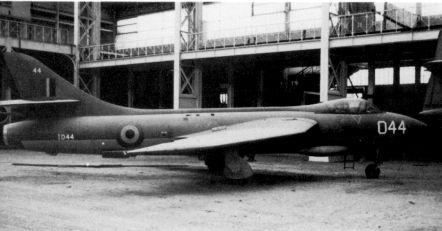

development was to rectify this failing, and the F.1 and F.2 were succeeded in production by the Hunter F.4 and the similar Sapphire-powered F.5, which had the internal fuel capacity increased from 334 to 414 Imp gals (1,518 to 1,882 litres) by additional fuel cells in the wing leading edges. In addition two underwing pylons were featured for 100-Imp gal (454-litres) Bristol drop tanks made of asbestos phenolic plastic, or for two 1,000-lb (454-kg) bombs. The first production Hunter F.4, WT701, first flew on 20 October 1954 and followed the

113th and last Kingston-built F.1. Altogether 365 of this mark were built, 188 at Kingston and 177 more (commencing WW646) at Squires Gate, deliveries beginning in March 1955. The first 159 British-built F.4s had the same Avon 113 engine as the F.1, but the 160th and later aircraft had the Avon 115 incorporating modifications intended to cure the surge problem, and some later aircraft had the Avon 121 turbojet. Later the 'dog tooth' wing leading edge extension first introduced late in the Hunter F.6 production run to cure pitch-up at high speeds and

Peruvian officers in front of one of the 16 Hunter F.52s delivered to the Fuerza Aerea del Peru from February 1956. These equipped *Escuadron* 14 of *Grupo* 12, based at Limatambo, and served until replaced in 1980 by Sukhoi Su-22s of Soviet design. Roundels and fin flash were red, white and red, and the serial 638 was in black.

altitudes was fitted retrospectively to most other surviving Hunters, including F.4s, during 1959-66. Another modification, also featured on a few F.1s, was the addition of rather large fairings on the fuselage under the Aden cannon to collect spent cartridge links and prevent them damaging the air brake or the rear fuselage. These bulges were called 'Sabrinas' after a well-developed film star of the 1950s.

At the 1955 Farnborough display Hunter F.4 WV385 did aerobatics with a 100-Imp gal (454-litres) Bristol drop tank under the port wing tip, another similar tank under the starboard wing, a 1,000-lb (454-kg) bomb under the main port underwing pylon and, under the starboard wing tip, three tiers of four 3-in (7.6-cm) rocket projectiles with 12-lb (5.4-kg) warheads on zero length launchers. Also at Farnborough that year in the static park was Hunter F.4 WT780 fitted with a nose having six ports for oblique, vertical and horizontal cameras; WT780 was later modified to carry a Cinemascope camera. At the 1956 SBAC Show Hunter F.4 XF310 did aerobatics with a Fairey Fireflash air-to-air guided missile under each wing on the pylon, the nose, which had a dielectric nose cap, being lengthened to house the Ecko radar for this beam-riding missile, code-named 'Blue Sky', which the RAF used in small numbers for training. Later a camera nose similar to that on F.4 WT780 was fitted to XF310, which was later converted into a T.7 trainer, one of six F.4s so converted during 1958-59. About 70 F.4s were also converted into T.8 and GA. Mk 11 trainers for the Royal Navy.

First deliveries of the Hunter F.4 were made to No 111 Squadron at North Weald, Essex, in June 1955 and No 54 Squadron at Odiham, Hampshire, in September; the former's F.4s, which replaced Meteor F.8s, served until November 1956 when they gave way to the Hunter F.6s with which 'Treble One' gained an international reputation for its formation aerobatic displays. No 54 Squadron's F.4s also gave way to Hunter F.6s at the beginning of 1957, and in April 1955 the first Hunters to be stationed overseas were the F.4s that re-equipped

No 98 Squadron with the 2nd Tactical Air Force in Germany, based at Jever. This mark went on to equip 19 more RAF squadrons, of which 12 were based in Germany and the rest in the UK; F.4s provided a major part of the 2nd TAF's fighter/ground attack strength.

First export customer for the Hunter was Sweden, which ordered 120 F.4s – designated Hunter F.Mk 50 in the export version – for the Royal Swedish Air Force, or Flygvapnet, who gave them the designation J 34. Deliveries of these began in August 1955 and the F.50s equipped the F 8, F 9, F 10 and F 18 *Flottiljer* (or Wings), F 8 being based at Barkaby, near Stockholm, F 9 at Säve, near Gothenburg, F 10 at Angelholm and F 18 at Tullinge, near Stockholm. Swedish Hunter F.50s were later modified to carry two Rb 324 (Sidewinder) infra-red air-to-air homing missiles on the underwing pylons. The last two Wings to operate the type were F 9 and F 10, which re-equipped with the Saab J 35 Draken in 1964 and 1967 respectively. The Royal Danish Air Force acquired 30 Hunter F.51s very similar to the F.4, deliveries beginning in January 1956. These equipped *Eskadrille* 724 (No 724 Squadron) and 16 of them were still in service in 1968, operating from their base at Skrydstrup exclusively in the lo-lo (low-level) intercept role. But early in 1974 the squadron was disbanded as part of defence cutbacks, and the Hunter F.51s were withdrawn from service, later being sold back to the manufacturers. In February 1956 deliveries began of 16 ex-RAF F.4s (now Hunter F.52s) to the Peruvian Air Force (Fuerza Aérea del Peru), one of the best equipped South American air arms. Here they equipped *Escuadron* 14, one of the three *Escuadrones de Caza* (or fighter squadrons) of *Grupo* 12, and remained in service for more than 20 years; the 10 surviving Hunters were still

operating in 1979, but not long after the squadron was disbanded and the type withdrawn.

Like the Gloster Meteor F.4 and F.8, the Hunter was also built under licence in Holland and Belgium from 1956, starting with the F.4; Fokker, with Aviolanda Maatschappij voor Vliegtuigbouw NV as subcontractors, produced 96 Hunter F.4s and 93 Hunter F.6s for the Royal Netherlands Air Force, and 112 F.4s and 52 F.6s for the Belgian Air Force. In addition, some assembly of Dutch-manufactured components was undertaken by Avions Fairey SA and SABCA in Belgium, a total of 128 sets of Fokker-built components being supplied for final assembly by these two firms, of which 92 were completed as or later converted to Hunter F.6s. Originally 396 Hunters were ordered for Dutch and Belgian production, but this was later reduced to 381 aircraft. Their Avon engines were built under licence in Belgium by the famous armament firm Fabrique Nationale d'Armes de Guerre, which had previously built Derwents for Dutch- and Belgian-built Meteors; these Avons corresponded to the Mk 113 and Mk 203 of British-built Hunters. Hunter F.4s and F.6s equipped six day-fighter squadrons of the Dutch Air Force, Nos 322 to 327, but by 1964 the last two of these had been disbanded. The Belgian Air Force took delivery of its first Hunter F.4s in the summer of 1956, these equipping Nos 7, 8 and 9 Squadrons of the 7th Wing, and also Nos 349, 350 and 4 Squadrons of the 1st Wing; they served only a short time with this wing as they were soon replaced by Avro Canada CF-100 Mk 5 all-weather fighters. Nos 22 and 26 Squadrons of the 9th Wing also had F.4s, and both these units and Nos 7 and 8 Squadrons of the 7th Wing later received Hunter F.6s. By 1963 the Belgian Air Force had a surplus of Hunters and some of these were flown back to England for refurbishing and resale to other air forces.

The Hunter F.6

Design work on the first major development of the Hunter, the Hawker P.1083 project, started in November 1951, only four months after the first prototype WB188 had made its maiden flight. The P.1083 was to be genuinely supersonic, capable of Mach 1.2 in level flight, and featured a thinner wing of only 6 per cent thickness/chord ratio and with a sharper sweepback of 50°. Powerplant was an RA.14R Avon with reheat and the P.1083 featured many other changes over the P.1067, including a flush-fitting fuselage air brake. Hunter WN470 was earmarked for conversion to the P.1083 prototype and conversion work was well under way when in June 1953 the whole project was turned down in favour of the Supermarine 545, which itself was cancelled later, in 1955. The decision not to go ahead with the P.1083 was partly based on the Air Staff's view that genuinely supersonic missile-carrying fighters would be available in about four years' time, but this decision proved to be a big mistake, as the P.1083 would have given the RAF an aircraft equal to or better than the F-100 Super Sabre and many other contemporary fighters, and with heavier attack loads. For a time Hawker also studied the still faster P.1091 delta wing fighter project with an afterburning Sapphire 4R turbojet, but in the end the next stage in Hunter development took the form of fitting the basic airframe with the 'large bore' Avon 200 series of 10,000 lb (4,540 kg) s.t. with a redesigned compressor and a 'cannular' combustion chamber.

This resulted in the Hawker P.1099 XF833, painted pale green, which served as the proto-type of the Hunter F.6 and first flew on 22 January 1954. It was completed in only three months by

the simple expedient of using the centre fuselage sub-assembly of the cancelled P.1083 WN470, and flight trials were satisfactory, although there were several engine failures, a couple of these being due to turbine blade failures. XF833 was later used for braking parachute trials and then by Rolls-Royce for thrust reverser testing. For the 1956 Farnborough display it was fitted with a smoke bottle in the tailpipe by Rolls to demonstrate the effect of thrust reversal; XF833 landed with a cloud of smoke trailing from the jet pipe, and when the thrust reverser was applied this cloud increased and enveloped the aircraft as it slowed to a halt. The jet efflux was directed outward and forward for reversal by a system of shutters and multiple cascade vanes. The Avon's thrust reverser was completely finalised during 1,000 hours of running and over 200 landings in XF833.

Like the F.4, the Hunter F.6 came on to the production line with less trouble than some of the intermediate modifications, and a contract for ten F.4s was changed to one for seven F.6s (from WW592 to WW598) which served as development aircraft for the new mark. WW592 was first flown by test pilot Bill Bedford on 25 March 1955, and the first true production F.6 was XE526, first flown by Hugh Merewether on 11 October 1955. With a 10,000-lb (4,540-kg) s.t. Avon 203, the F.6 had a much improved performance and a greatly increased take-off weight, and the first F.6 deliveries to Maintenance Units began in January 1956. But three problems were encountered which delayed the new mark's acceptance for squadron service until October that year; the first and probably most serious of these was the onset of severe pitch-up at high speeds and high altitudes. By contrast pitch-down occurred when the guns were fired at high altitudes, and this problem was cured by developing and fitting muzzle blast deflectors. In investigating this

problem one Hunter fired a total of 40,000 rounds in flight at full throttle. The third problem was the development of a full-power elevator; flight trials with a ram air turbine in the rear fuselage to operate a slab tailplane started in 1956, and this turbine was fitted to the Hunter F.4 WT780 which had a camera nose. But in the end fully-powered elevators with spring feel and different linkage were

The formation loop by 22 Hunters of the 'Black Arrows' at the 1958 Farnborough display; the number of aircraft in this loop is thought to be still a record.

increased the wing area from 340 sq ft (31.5 m^2) to 349 sq ft (32.4 m^2). The 'dog tooth' leading edges were first fitted to F.6 XJ632 about three-quarters of the way through the F.6 production run, and they were fitted retrospectively to all preceding F.6s and to the majority of surviving Hunters, mostly F.4s and T.7s, from 1959 to 1966. Meanwhile the first 100 or so production F.6s without the muzzle blast deflectors and leading edge extensions were delivered to the squadrons and flown for a time under temporary restrictions, while modification kits to update them were produced and issued to RAF units.

The first unit to re-equip with Hunter F.6s was No 74 (F) Squadron at Horsham St Faith, Norfolk, which moved to Coltishall in the same county in June 1959; No 74's F.6s were replaced by Lightning F.1s in November 1960. By March 1957 production of F.6s was about 40 aircraft a month, and the planned build-up rate of two F.6 squadrons a month was being achieved, with Nos 43, 54, 63, 92, 247 and 263 Squadrons as well as No 74(F) re-equipped with the new mark or completing delivery of their F.6s, plus No 111 Squadron by the end of 1957. The 2nd TAF squadrons in Germany were also re-equipped with F.6s which, by 1958, equipped all the RAF day fighter squadrons in Europe. In March 1958 the first F.6s joined the Middle East Air Force when No 208 Squadron, which had taken over No 34 Squadron's Hunter F.5s at Tangmere when that unit was disbanded, flew the latter to Cyprus and also introduced F.6s at the same time, operating these until it was disbanded on 30 March 1959. On 14 July 1958 there was a Russian-backed revolution in Iraq in which King Faisal and the Prime Minister were

murdered, and the brief Arab Federation between Iraq and Jordan which the King had headed ended. To protect Jordan from an Iraqi-backed takeover, British paratroops were airlifted to Jordan from Cyprus from 17 July in Blackburn Beverley C.1s escorted by No 208 Squadron Hunters.

In addition to the squadrons, Hunter F.6s were also used by Nos 229 and 233 OCUs at Chivenor, Devon, and Pembrey, Carmarthen, respectively and also by the Fighter Weapons School, the Central Flying School, the Central Fighter Establishment and the Empire Test Pilots' School. No 229 OCU continued to fly Hunter F.6s until the early 1970s, and late in 1974 this OCU and its Hunters moved from Chivenor to a new base at Brawdy in Pembrokeshire, at the same time changing its name to No 1 Tactical Weapons Unit. About this time some of the Hunter F.6s were modified up to FGA.9 standard and in this form were known as Hunter F.6As, while the remaining F.6s were fitted with FGA.9-type braking parachutes. No 1 TWU still flew 20 Hunter F.6s and F.6As in 1980, plus T.7s and FGA.9s, but they were gradually replaced by Hawk T.1s and only eight F.6As were still in service at the beginning of 1983. Altogether 19 squadrons operated Hunter F.6s of which five, Nos 4, 14, 20, 26 and 93, were based in Germany, No 208 in Cyprus and the rest were home-based.

Of the latter, the most famous was undoubtedly No 111 Squadron, based at North Weald, Essex, and – from June 1958 – at Wattisham, Suffolk, whose F.6s first appeared in their all-black colour scheme as the 'Black Arrows' in April 1957 as Fighter Command's aerobatic team. They set superlative standards in this field, and their formation loop with 22 Hunters at the 1958 Farnborough show will long be remembered; the number of aircraft in the loop is still thought to be a record to this day. As Air

adopted, and in 1957 production Hunter F.6s began to feature a 'flying tail' with the power-operated elevator interconnected to change the tailplane incidence electrically.

The pitch-up problem was cured by fitting extended and drooped (or 'dog tooth') leading edges to the outer wings, in which a large vortex was generated at the inboard end by a 'dog tooth' discontinuity; these extensions

WW594, seen here, was the first of two P.1109A Hunters and served as the aerodynamic test vehicle for the nose radar of P.1109B XF378, although the radar was not fitted. XF378 proved to be the fastest Hunter of all in 'clean' condition.

Vice-Marshal Peter Latham, who had taken over from Squadron Leader Roger Topp as the CO of 'Treble One' and who devised this manoeuvre, later recalled in an interview for *Pilot* magazine's October 1984 issue: 'I worked on the principle that formation aerobatics was like sex; there had to be a climax but it had to be at the end'. This big formation loop was very dependent on the weather for its proper execution, and was not repeated. Originally the 'Treble One' Hunters had a smoke canister under each wing tip, but this was soon changed to one in the jet pipe, and for the BBC's television coverage of the 1959 Farnborough display two of the F.6s were fitted with a Vinten 16 mm cine camera in their fins.

In 1961 No 92 Squadron took over from 'Treble One' as Fighter Command's aerobatic team, being known as the 'Blue Diamonds' from the royal blue (with white fuselage flash and wing tips) in which their Hunter F.6s were painted. The No 92 team derived its name from the diamond nine formation that was their hallmark, and their team usually included one or two Hunter T.7s. No 92's F.6s were replaced by Lightning F.2s and F.2As in April 1963 as were those of No 19 Squadron the previous November, and with the F.6s' departure from these two units this mark of Hunter was

phased out of Fighter Command. The last F.6s in service in Germany, with No 14 Squadron, were withdrawn when that unit disbanded on 17 December 1962, to be immediately succeeded by a new No 14 Squadron created by renumbering No 88 Squadron at Wildenrath; this flew Canberra B(I).8s until disbanded on 30 June 1970. The F.6s of the old No 14 Squadron had been the only day fighters in the 2nd TAF since January 1961.

As well as the day interceptor role, the Hunter F.6 was also excellent in ground attack and could carry a wide variety of loads under the four underwing pylons, in addition to the 100-Imp gal (454-litres) Bristol plastic drop tanks and 1,000-lb (454-kg) bombs of the Hunter F.4. The F.6 could also carry two 230-Imp gal (1,045-litres) mild steel drop tanks of Hawker manufacture on the inner pylons, the flaps being cut away to avoid fouling these tanks, which could be jettisoned with the aid of a cartridge, and with these and two 100-Imp gal (454-litres) drop tanks the F.6 could fly non-stop from Malta to Cyprus.

The big 230-Imp gal (1,045-litres) drop tanks, originally proposed before the Suez action of 1956, were intended to enable F.6s to fly from the UK to the Middle East non-stop. A pair of dummy tanks of this size were test

flown on a Hunter F.4, and on 2 October 1958 Hugh Merewether flew Hunter F.6 XF374 with two prototype 230-Imp gal (1,045 litres) and two 100-Imp gal (454-litres) drop tanks non-stop from Dunsfold to El Adem in Libya in 3 hours 19 minutes for the distance of 1,826 miles (2,938 km). Four 100 gal (454 litres) napalm tanks could also be carried, although no Hunter ever used these in action, and in 1956 F.6 XG131 was fitted as a trial installation with two fixed metal 85-Imp gal (386-litres) wing tip tanks. These were permanently attached by a finely faired sleeve over the normal wing tips, and each tank had a pitot head and navigation light fitted in it. These tip tanks were devised for possible application to the projected two-seater night/all-weather fighter variants of the Hunter, the Hawker P.1114 and P.1115, which were not built. These tanks resulted in quite unacceptable buffet conditions in flight, however, and XG131 was later converted back to a standard F.6 and was delivered to No 14 Squadron in Germany. As well as 1,000-lb (454-kg) bombs, 500-lb (227-kg) bombs and two small 25-lb (11.3-kg) practice bombs on carriers for pylon attachment the Hunter F.6 could also – for foreign air forces – carry four 400-kg or 200-kg bombs.

A wide variety of rocket projectiles could be carried, a typical installation being 4 tiers of three 3-in (76-mm) rockets under each outer wing and 2 tiers of three under each inner pylon, all attached to the standard Mk 12 launcher rails. These rockets could have a variety of warheads, from 25 lb (11.3 kg) to 60 lb (27.2 kg) in weight, and high explosive, armour-piercing or fragmentation in character. Export variants of the Hunter F.6 have been fitted with Oerlikon, Hispano, T.10 or Bofors rocket projectiles and rails, while HVAR and 'Tiny Tim' 5-in (127-mm) rockets could also be carried. The F.6 was also cleared to carry two rocket pods each carrying 37 2-in (50.8-mm) spin-stabilised unguided folding fin rockets, and a similar pod carrying 24 2-in (50.8-mm) rockets could also be carried. One Hunter F.6 did firing trials with the Fairey Fireflash (code-named 'Blue Sky') beam-riding air-to-air missile, one being carried under each wing, and several other F.6s were used for various special trials at the RAE Farnborough, Boscombe Down and Bedford.

F.6s XE587 and XE588 were demonstrated to the Swiss Air Force in 1957 in gunnery and bombing trials, this leading to the Swiss order for 100 Hunter F.6s (redesignated F.58s) in January 1958, and for this task XE587 was fitted with a tail braking ' parachute as a trial installation, as the Swiss had specified, and two 230-Imp gal (1,045-litres) and two 100-Imp gal (454-litres) drop tanks. XE587 also carried the badge of the Swiss Alpine Club, and it was later delivered to the Indian Air Force. Armstrong Whitworth-built Hunter F.6 XF378, also known as the Hawker P.1109B, was fitted with AI Mk 20 radar in a sharply pointed

nose and carried a de Havilland Firestreak air-to-air missile under each wing; only two 30-mm Aden cannon were carried, and the P.1109B proved to be the fastest Hunter of them all in 'clean' condition, faster even than the world speed record-breaking prototype WB188 in its F.3 form. The possibilities of a missile-carrying Hunter, perhaps based on the two-seater T.7, were never really explored, and the P.1109B later became a Hunter FGA.9. The AI Mk 20 radar proved to be troublesome, and a battle camera in a small protruding fairing was mounted on top of the nose above it and behind it. There were also two Hawker P.1109As very similar to the P.1109B but without radar; the first was WW594, which was an aerodynamic test vehicle for the revised nose but without the radar or missiles. WW598 was the second P.1109A and this was later used by the RAE's High Speed Flight for low-altitude gust investigation at high speeds in the Middle East to provide gust data for the BAC TSR-2 then being designed. Hunter F.6 XF379 was fitted with experimental lateral speed brakes in the rear fuselage,

but these did not become a standard feature.

The Korean War ended in 1953, the year that the first production Hunter F.1 and F.2 had first flown, and production, which had been geared up for this conflict, gradually lost impetus. The ill-conceived 1957 White Paper on Defence heralded a change-over from manned aircraft to guided missiles, but failed to foresee that continual 'brush fire' wars in the Middle and Far East would mean a continued need for fighter bombers for use in the ground-attack role. This White Paper, an over-reaction to the political failure of the Suez campaign, put paid to further major developments of the Hunter, and in July 1957 the most recent batches of 150 F.6s

A Hunter F.6 with the wide variety of external weapon loads it can carry. Just in front of the nosewheel is the 30-mm Aden gun pack with ammunition, and in the foreground are 1,000-lb (454-kg), 500-lb (227-kg) and 25-lb (11.3-kg) practice bombs, and 230-Imp gal (1,045-litre) and 100-Imp gal (454-litre) drop tanks. To the left by the gun pack is a row of 3-in (76-mm) rocket projectiles, while to the right is a row of spin-stabilised folding fin rockets and the rocket pods they are fired from. Under the wing tips are Fireflash and DH Firestreak air-to-air missiles.

This formation shot shows (from the top) Hunter F.6 XE587 fitted with a tail-braking parachute for demonstration to the Swiss Air Force in 1957; Hunter F.6 XK148 with rocket projectiles under the wings; P.1109B Hunter XF378 with AI Mk 20 radar in the sharply pointed nose and a DH Firestreak air-to-air missile under each wing; and Hunter F.4 XF310 with Ecko radar in the nose and a Fireflash missile under each wing.

ordered from Kingston (from XK225) and Coventry (from XJ945) were cancelled, and production at Squires Gate and by Armstrong Whitworth at Coventry ceased. Hawker built a total of 264 Hunter F.6s, the last of these to be built, XK156, being delivered on 9 July 1957, and Armstrong Whitworth built 119 F.6s (serialled XE581 to XG168), bringing total British production of F.6s to 415, of which 383 were for the RAF. Thirty-two F.6s were exported in 1957-58, 15 to the Iraqi Air Force, 12 to the Royal Jordanian Air Force and five to the Lebanese Air Force (Force

Aérienne Libanaise); unlike later deliveries these did not receive export mark numbers in the F.50s range. One of the Jordanian F.6s, serialled 712, was later converted to F.R.6 standard for tactical reconnaissance, with three cameras in the nose.

In addition, 93 F.6s were built by Fokker and Aviolanda in Holland for the Royal Netherlands Air Force, and 52 F.6s for the Belgian Air Force, with a further 92 completed as F.6s from Fokker-built components or later converted to F.6s by Avions Fairey SA and SABCA in Belgium. Dutch and Belgian production of the F.6 began in 1958, and this mark equipped Nos 7 and 8 Squadrons of the Belgian Air Force's 7th Wing at Chièvres, each with 25 aircraft, and Nos 22 and 26 Squadrons of the 9th Wing. The 9th Wing was converted in 1962 to operate Nike-Ajax and Nike-Hercules ground-to-air missiles, and in 1964 the 7th Wing re-equipped

with F–104G Starfighters. Hunter F.6s also equipped the Belgian Air Force aerobatic team, 'Les Diables Rouges'. In Dutch Air Force service Hunter F.4s and F.6s equipped six day-fighter squadrons, Nos 322, 323 and 324 at Leeuwarden, No 325 at Soesterberg and Nos 326 and 327 at Twente. No 322 Squadron also served for a time at Biak in Dutch New Guinea, but this territory was seized in 1963 by Indonesia and became West Irian. By 1963 Nos 326 and 327 Squadrons were disbanded, and later Nos 322 and 323 re-equipped with F–104G Starfighters, while No 324 became a missile unit. The Hunter F.6s of No 325 were later equipped with two Sidewinder infra-red homing missiles, and the last Dutch F.6 was withdrawn from first-line service with this unit at the end of 1966; a few F.6s remained in service for target towing.

For a while British production of the basic F.6 to export orders, such as the F.56 for India and the F.58 for Switzerland, continued, but all later Hunter deliveries of factory-new aircraft were two-seater trainers, later single-seater marks such as the FGA.9, F.R.10 and G.A.11 being conversions of F.6s and F.4s. By December 1957 the RAF had 210 F.6s on first-line strength, with a further 159 at Maintenance Units plus 14 more crashed or written off.

Not only were the F.6s cancelled in July 1957 not built but, with tragic lack of foresight, large numbers of potentially saleable earlier marks were broken up at Maintenance Units, often after only a few hours flying time. However, some F.6s were saved from this fate for resale and export, the first 12 for India being ex-RAF ones returned from MUs, being followed by 32 more for that country from the last cancelled batch of RAF F.6s (XK157-XK176 and XK213-XK224, these becoming BA201-BA232 with the Indian Air Force). By 1963 about 30 ex-Belgian Air Force F.6s had been acquired by Hawker, most being flown back to

Dunsfold with Hawker's G–9 prefixed Class B registrations and the Belgian insignia deleted. These were refurbished and modified up to FGA.9 standards, 18 being resold to Iraq and four to Kuwait during 1963-4. More low time Belgian and Dutch F.6s were flown back to Hawker for similar refurbishing and resale, and many more F.6s were later refurbished at Kingston.

Hunters in Indian Service

After three months' evaluation of the Hunter in this country by Indian pilots in the summer of 1957, an order was placed for 160 Hunter F.6s for the Indian Air Force on 1 September, 1957. Eventually 32 of the last cancelled RAF batch for 150, completed as F.56s were delivered to the Indian Air Force. The Indian Hunters were ferried out to Karachi, each with four 100-Imp gal (454-litres) drop tanks, deliveries beginning in October 1957 and continuing until February 1961. The 49th and subsequent Hunter F.56s were fitted with a 10-ft 6-in (3.20-m) diameter ring-slot braking parachute in the tail similar to that of the FGA.9. The F.56s equipped Nos 7, 14, 17, 20 and 27 Squadrons of the Indian Air Force based at Poona and Ambala. They first saw action in 1961 when India seized the small Portuguese coastal enclave of Goa, about 300 miles (483 km) down the coast from Bombay.

In 1965 war broke out between India and Pakistan over the mountain state of Kashmir, which had for years been a bone of contention between the two countries. In April that year fighting broke out on the disputed border in the Rann of Kutch, but a cease-fire was arranged on 1 July. Not long afterwrads large numbers of Pakistani irregulars crossed the cease-fire line into Indian Kashmir; by 5 August India was claiming that a 'full-blooded' invasion had occurred, and on 24 August the Indians sent troops in strength across the cease-fire line. In return

Pakistan launched an offensive on 1 September in the Chhamb sector with an infantry brigade and 70 tanks, and both countries' air forces played an important part in the ensuing three weeks' war, which ended when a cease-fire came into effect on 23 September. During this period the Indians claimed 73 Pakistan Air Force aircraft destroyed in the air and by AA fire for the loss of 35 of their own, while the Pakistanis claimed 110 Indian aircraft destroyed, of which 35 were destroyed by their Air Force in combat and 43 on the ground, while a further 32 fell victim to ground fire; the Pakistanis admitted the loss of only 16 aircraft, of which all but two were F–86F Sabres.

On 3 September two Pakistani Air Force Sabres intercepted six Indian Hunters and Gnats over the Bhimber area, shooting down a Gnat over Pakistani territory and badly damaging two of the Hunters, which came down in Indian-held Kashmir. Three days later Indian troops launched a three-pronged attack against Lahore to forestall a Pakistani invasion of the Punjab. The 6th was a day of fierce fighting on land and in the air, in which Pakistani Sabres claimed eight Indian Hunters in fighter sweeps over IAF bases, including Halwara and Adampur, for the loss of two Sabres, while the Indians claimed all four Sabres attacking Halwara shot down, three by Hunters and one by AA fire. The Indians also claimed another flight of four Sabres from East Pakistan that attacked Kalaikunda in the eastern sector, two being shot down by Hunters and two by AA fire.

One of the fiercest air battles of the war took place on 7 September over the Pakistani Air Force base of Sargodha, which was attacked by Hunters, Gnats and Mystères; during the fighting Squadron Leader Mohammad Mahmud Alam in his Sabre shot down five Hunters in a fight lasting barely a minute. He had already claimed four Hunters in earlier encounters,

and for his exploits was awarded the Sitara-e-Jurat (Pakistani DFC) and bar. The Indian Air Force did plenty of ground-attack work during this war, and on 8 September four Hunters attacked and destroyed with rocket projectiles a goods train in Raiwind station; having left the train ablaze and exploding, they flew on to attack Pakistani ground forces near Kasur, accounting for four tanks and 30 vehicles. It later transpired that the goods train was carrying petrol and ammunition for the Pakistani tanks in the Khem Karan area and, with the train's destruction, the Pakistani armour had to go into battle with only 30 shells for each tank, and low on fuel supplies; when their initial thrust was stopped by the Indian armour, the Pakistani tanks had to withdraw with heavy losses. On 20 September the UN Security Council called for a cease-fire, which took effect on the 23rd.

To make up for attrition and losses incurred in the war, the Indian Air Force took delivery of 36 refurbished Hunter F.56As and 12 T.66D two-seater trainers between June 1966 and September 1967, the F.56As being ex-Belgian Air Force and the T.66Ds ex-Dutch; 13 more F.56As and at least one T.66D were acquired about six years later. The Hunters acquired in 1966-67 were ferried out in batches of four accompanied by an Indian Air Force Canberra B(I).58 which acted as a navigation lead ship. By 1979 about 130 Hunter F.56s, F.56As and T.66s were still in service, equipping four ground-attack squadrons, Nos 14, 20, 27 and 37, but with first deliveries of the Jaguar International, the Hunters and Canberras are at last being withdrawn from service, and both types are being put up for sale; British Aerospace are to acquire some Indian Hunters for refurbishing. Somewhat belatedly the Indian Air Force formed a Hunter aerobatic team, known as 'The Thunderbolts', late in 1981, flying six aircraft (later to be nine) from its base at Hasimara.

F.6 Exports and Refurbishing

First export customer for the Hunter F.6, apart from Holland and Belgium with their own production of the type, was Iraq, to whom the British Government presented 15 Hunter F.6s from RAF stocks, five in April 1957 and ten in December that year. These supplemented the Iraqi Air Force's DH Venom F.B.50s and Vampire F.B.52s but not long after their delivery, a Russian-backed revolution occurred in July 1958 in which General Kassem seized power and King Faisal II and the royal family were murdered, a republic being proclaimed. A succession of anti-western Baathist regimes followed, with shifts towards and away from Soviet bloc influence, and this led to re-equipment of the Air Force with MiG–21s, MiG–19s MiG–15s and other Russian types. But the Hunter and other British types remained in service, even the piston-engined Hawker Fury being used in close-support operations against the rebels in Kurdistan, who wanted autonomy from the Baghdad government. When General Kassem's forces were in revolt against the King, Hunter F.6s flown by rebel pilots from Mosul made rocket attacks against royalist encampments in southern Iraq, and this is thought to be the first time the Hunter actually fired its weapons in anger.

The first 15 F.6s equipped one fighter/bomber squadron, and these were supplemented by a further batch of 18 F.6s ordered in 1963, deliveries of which began late in 1964. These, with the new 'export' mark number Hunter F.59, were refurbished from the first batch of 32 ex-Belgian Air Force F.6s flown back during late 1962 and early 1963 to Hawker's at Dunsfold for conversion to FGA.9

standard and resale. A further 26 F.6s were similarly refurbished and updated for Iraq as Hunter F.59s from the second batch of 64 ex-Belgian F.6s flown back to Dunsfold in late 1964 and early 1965; these, delivered to Iraq during 1965-66, made 44 altogether, and the first 26 of these had the Iraqi serials 568 to 587 and 626 to 631. By 1966 the Iraqi Air Force had four Hunter squadrons, and had also acquired four Hunter F.R.10s for tactical reconnaissance in addition to the F.59s. In the early and mid-1970s Iraq acquired further Soviet aircraft of more modern types, followed more recently by Dassault Mirage F.1EQs and Super Etendards, but 30 of the Hunter F.59s and F.R.10s still remain in service in three strike squadrons.

In addition to Iraq, the British Government also presented Hunter F.6s to both Jordan and the Lebanon at about the same time. The Royal Arab Air Force, as Jordan's small defensive air arm was then known, received 12 initially and the Force Aérienne Libanaise five. The Jordanian ones equipped one day-interceptor squadron, and one of these Hunters, serialled 712, was later modified to F.R.6 standard with three cameras in the nose for tactical reconnaissance; this variant was similar to the Hunter F.R.10 but did not have the tail-braking parachute. It did have two 230-Imp gal (1,045-litres) and two 100-Imp gal (454-litres) drop tanks, but the big tanks, unlike those of RAF F.6s, were not stressed for combat loads. In 1963 four Jordanian pilots defected to Egypt in their Hunter F.6s, but these were apparently returned to Jordan by the Egyptians. Later more refurbished Hunters were acquired to replace the original F.6s, and by 1973 two Jordanian fighter/bomber squadrons were equipped with 32 Hunter FGA.73As and 73Bs, but in 1975 all but one of these were acquired by the Sultan of Oman's Air Force when the Royal

Jordanian Air Force re-equipped with Northrop F–5s.

The Force Aérienne Libanaise later added five Hunter FGA.9s and two Hunter T.66 trainers to the five originally donated by Britain, and the dozen Hunters equipped one operational day-fighter squadron, also being used in the ground-attack role. In 1975 a further six Hunter F.70s were ordered to make up for earlier losses, and by 1978 17 of this variant had been acquired, of which eight were still in service early in 1983, although three were lost in action in August and September that year. The bitter civil war in the Lebanon, not perhaps surprising in a country with so many rival Christian and Muslim religious sects and with more than 20 political organisations, has offered little scope for conventional air power. But towards the end of 1983 Lebanese Air Force Hunters were in action for the first time against the Druze forces, the latter being one of the three large Muslim groups, with their heartland in southeastern Lebanon. Five Hunters operated against them for a time using a road strip near Biblis.

Kuwait, in spite of its large oil revenues, had only a modest air force, partly because for a long time there was only one military air base in the country, which shared the two runways used by the major international civil airport. The Kuwaiti Air Force, an extension of the Security Department of the Government of Kuwait, was advised and trained in its formative years by an RAF mission. Its first jet equipment consisted of four Hunter F.57s, serialled from 210 to 213, that were refurbished and updated to FGA.9 standards from ex-Belgian Air Force F.6s. They were delivered late in 1964 in high gloss mid-stone and dark earth camouflage, with azure blue undersides, and were supplemented by two Hunter T.67 two-seat trainers, a further three T.67s being acquired later. These equipped one ground-attack squadron but by 1978 the F.57s had been retired from use and only the five T.67s were in service; these have now been withdrawn as they have been replaced in the strike role by McDonnell Douglas A–4KU Skyhawks.

The first Hunter F.6s for Iraq, Jordan and the Lebanon had been gifts from the British Government, but the first country to place a true export order for the F.6 was India (see previous chapter). Just before the first refurbished Hunters for India were delivered in 1966, the Royal Saudi Air Force took delivery of four ex-RAF Hunter F.6s, serialled 60-601 to 60-604, and two Hunter T.7s, serialled 70-616 and 70-617, in May and June 1966. These were used to provide jet experience and ground-attack training for Saudi pilots pending delivery of the 34 Lightning F.53s and six Lightning T.55 two-seat trainers ordered by the Saudis early in 1966. These Hunters did not have an export mark number, and were finished in light earth and dark earth camouflage with azure blue undersides; the roundels and fin flash were green and white, and serials and other lettering were emerald green.

Switzerland was the second country after India to place an export order for the Hunter F.6, to meet a new fighter requirement; after considering the Canadair CL–13 Sabre, the Folland Gnat and Switzerland's own indigenous fighter design, the FFA P–16, which had become the first Swiss type to exceed Mach 1 in August 1956, the Hunter was chosen and an order for 100 was placed in January 1958, with the export mark number F.58. The first 12 Hunters delivered to Switzerland were released from RAF stocks of the F.6, and the remaining 88 Hunter F.58s were completed to FGA.9 standards, with tail-braking parachutes and muzzle blast deflectors. Deliveries to Switzerland started in April 1958 and continued until 1960, the Hunters equipping five *Flieger-*

Top: 60–602, seen here, was one of four Hunter F.6s and two T.7s supplied to the Royal Saudi Air Force in 1966.

Above: One of the four Hunter F.57s delivered to the Kuwaiti Air Force late in 1964 and refurbished from ex-Belgian F.6s.

staffeln, or squadrons, and being serialled J–4001 to J–4100. Early in 1971 it was announced that a further 30 Hunters refurbished to F.58A standard would be acquired, these being converted from ex-RAF F.6s, and at the same time eight Hunter T.68 trainers were supplied to Switzerland, which had not operated the two-seater variant before. A further 22 Hunter

F.58As were later supplied, and the final assembly of the 60 refurbished Hunter F.58As and T.68s, and the application of Swiss Air Force modifications to them, was subcontracted by Hawker Siddeley to the Swiss Federal Aircraft Factory, or F + W as it was also known, at its Emmen works. The Hunter F.58As were serialled J–4101 to J–4152, and the T.68s

J–4201 to J–4208; their delivery was spread over several years from the autumn of 1972, the last one being delivered to the Swiss Air Force on 8 July 1976.

Hawker Siddeley had originally proposed a variant known as the Super Hunter to the Swiss in 1970–71 to meet their requirements; this featured an increased war load, greater fuel capacity and thrust, a more accurate and comprehensive weapon system and higher-energy wheel brakes. The Super Hunter, which was also known by the Swiss designation Hunter S.2 minus, would have had only two 30-mm Aden cannon but additional strong points to allow the simultaneous carrying of up to four 1,000-lb (454-kg) bombs, two 230-Imp gals (1,045-litres) drop tanks and two Sidewinder air-to-air missiles. An alternative load would have been eight 1,000-lb (454-kg) bombs and two Sidewinders, and ejection release units were designed into the pylons to ensure positive separation of bombs and tanks under all flight conditions. A laser range unit incorporated in the Saab BT9R bombing system provided more accurate weapon aiming, and a GGS Mk 8 gun sight and radar ranging was fitted for air-to-air firing of the cannons and Sidewinders. But in the end the Swiss turned down the Super Hunter in favour of refurbished Hunter F.58As.

By 1979 there were 148 Hunters in the Swiss inventory, and they are now equipped with Saab BT9K bombing computers and armed with Sidewinder air-to-air missiles. They are currently being further updated with radar-warning receivers and the necessary electronics to carry the AGM–65 Maverick air-to-ground missile, of which 500 have been ordered, and some of the T.68s are now used in the ECM (electronics countermeasures) role. Hunters now equip nine *staffeln* in the ground-attack role, and one of these units, with others equipped

with the Dassault Mirage III and IIIRS and Northrop F–5Es, forms part of the Surveillance Wing for air defence.

When it became clear that Britain was going to withdraw its military presence from the Persian (or Arabian) Gulf, several of the Gulf states which had previously enjoyed British protection started to form their own air arms. Among these was Abu Dhabi, which chose refurbished Hunters for its Defence Force Air Wing in 1969, ten Hunter FGA.76s and F.R.76As, serialled 701 to 710, and two Hunter T.77 trainers, serialled 711 and 712, being supplied for the Air Wing's Fighter Flight; the F.R.76A had cameras in the nose. The first two Hunters, a Mk 76 and a Mk 76A, were handed over at Dunsfold early in 1970 with two 230-Imp gal (1,045-litres) and two 100-Imp gal (454-litres) drop tanks for the delivery flight to Abu Dhabi. One Hunter, serial 708, was lost in an accident in 1970 and a second crashed later. The Hunters were finished in light sand and dark earth camouflage with light blue undersurfaces. With the arrival of the first six Dassault Mirage 5s for Abu Dhabi, the Hunters were detached on a rotational basis to defend the neighbouring emirate of Sharjah, returning to Abu Dhabi for major servicing, which was carried out for the Defence Force Air Wing's aircraft under contract by Airwork Services until March 1974.

On 2 December 1971 the United Arab Emirates was formed as a federation of seven Gulf states: Abu Dhabi, Dubai, Sharjah, Ajman, Fujairah, Ras Al-Khaimah and Umm Al-Quwain; Sheikh Zayed of Abu Dhabi was the driving force behind the formation of the UAE. Its air arm was started as the Union Defence Force Air Wing with three Agusta-Bell AB 206A JetRanger helicopters donated by Abu Dhabi, and in October 1974 it was renamed the Union Air Force. This was later amalgamated with Abu Dhabi's air arm and the Dubai Police Air Wing

to form the United Emirates Air Force, with Abu Dhabi's air arm forming by far the largest single part. As the Mirage force built up to its full strength of 32 aircraft, the Hunters, now used in the ground-attack role, were based permanently on Sharjah. They served until 1983 when, with the arrival of 16 Hawk T.63 trainers for Abu Dhabi and eight Hawk T.61s for Dubai, the Hunters were withdrawn from use and passed on to the Somali Aeronautical Corps, to supplement the latter's MiG–21s and MiG–17s which, with other Russian types, had mostly become unserviceable.

Qatar, like Bahrain, remained outside the United Arab Emirates when this was formed, but became independent on 1 September 1971. Three Hunter FGA.78s and a Hunter T.79 trainer were acquired for the Qatar Emiri Air Force, being refurbished Dutch Air Force aircraft, and they were based at Doha. They were maintained and flown by British personnel, and mainly used for regular coastal patrols; one of the FGA.78s was lost in a crash in 1977. The Hunters remain in service even though Qatar is now taking delivery of 14 Dassault Mirage F.1Es and F.1Bs and six Alpha Jets. In 1975 the neighbouring Sultanate of Oman acquired 31 Hunter FGA.73As and 73Bs from the Royal Jordanian Air Force when the latter re-equipped with Northrop F–5s, and they equipped No 6 Squadron of the Sultan of Oman's Air Force at its main strike base of Thumrayt. Only about 15 of the Hunters were operational at any one time, the remainder being stored, and by 1983 there were 14 in service, including one F.R.10. They had been fitted with AIM–9P Sidewinder air-to-air

Right: The RA.21 Avon engine of this Hunter instructional airframe, with the maintenance serial 7519M, is withdrawn from the fuselage, the detached rear fuselage and tail being in the background. This Avon variant has eight combustion chambers and a 12-stage compressor.

Above: Hunter F.6A XF516:19 of No 1 Tactical Weapons Unit. The F.6A is an F.6 modified up to FGA.9 standards; note 'pen nib' fairing for tail-braking parachute at base of rudder.

Above, centre: A Hunter T.7 of No 1 Tactical Weapons Unit climbs out after taking off.

Far right, top: This attractively finished red-and-white Hunter T.7 XL577:82 belongs to No 1 Tactical Weapons Unit.

Far right, middle: Hunter T.7 XL617:95, seen here, was later coded 89 with No 1 TWU and has recently become an instructional airframe at RAF Scampton with the serial 8837M.

Right: Sapphire-engined Hunter F.5 7583M:E at RAF Henlow in 1970.

Main picture: Three Hunter FGA.9s, XE546:N, XE552:R and XG157:H, of No 2 Tactical Weapons Unit with 230-Imp gal (1,045-litre) drop tanks.

Inset above: Hunter FGA.9 XF435:52 of No 1 Tactical Weapons Unit's No 79 Squadron with 230-Imp gal (1,045-litre) drop tanks. This Hunter is now fitted for target towing.

Inset left: Royal Navy Hunter T.7 XF321:728 seen here at RNAS Yeovilton in July 1972 was one of five Hunter F.4s converted to T.7s.

Left: Seen about to take off at the 1960 SBAC Show is Hunter F.R.10 XG168 with 230-Imp gal (1,045-litre) and 100-Imp gal (454-litre) drop tanks.

Centre: Hunter GA.11 WW654:833 was one of the 'Blue Herons' aerobatic team operated by the Fleet Requirements and Direction Unit (FRADU) at Yeovilton. This team was the only one in which military jets were flown by civilian pilots.

Below: Hunter F.50 34016:06 of the Royal Swedish Air Force. The F.50, designed J34 by the Swedes, was an export variant of the F.4.

Right: A formation shot of five Swiss Air Force Hunter F.58s.

Below: Swiss Air Force Hunter F.58 J–4028 (foreground) and another seen taking off. Switzerland now has the world's largest inventory of Hunters.

missiles for air defence, and could carry BL–755 cluster bombs and other ground-attack weapons.

Most refurbished Hunter sales were to Middle East and Asian countries, but a notable exception was Chile, which took delivery of a total of 30 Hunter FGA.71s, three Hunter F.R.71As with a camera nose and four Hunter T.72 trainers, these being delivered in batches from 1967. These replaced the Fuerza Aerea de Chile's Lockheed F–80C Shooting Stars, and equipped two Grupos Aereos (Air Groups), each made up of one Escuadrilla (Squadron); these were Grupo 7 at Los Cerillos and Grupo 9 at Puerto Montt. In 1973 Chile underwent a revolution in which the Marxist President Allende was overthrown and a right-wing regime headed by General Pinochet took over the country; Hunters took part in the fighting preceding the President's overthrow. The new regime faced opposition from European socialist parties, including Britain's Labour government, which for several years prevented the supply of spares and engine and airframe overhauls for the Hunters. In June 1978 the Chileans officially admitted that due to lack of spares only 20 Hunters were still flying. After the Falklands conflict and Chile's covert assistance to Britain relations between the two countries improved considerably, one consequence being that seven more Hunter FGA.9s from No 1 TWU at Brawdy were refurbished and supplied to Chile from July 1982 as Mk 71s to make up for past attrition and losses, while at

Above left: Hunter FGA.74:535 of the Singapore Air Defence Command, which started life as F.6 XE599 and became G–9–376. This Hunter was one of two FGA.74s and two T.75s based with No 1 TWU at Brawdy for a time for training Singaporean pilots.

Left: Hawker's well-known scarlet-and-white Hunter T.66A demonstrator G–APUX was perhaps the most aesthetically pleasing of all Hunters. It was put through a 12-turn spin by Bill Bedford at the 1959 and 1960 Farnborough displays.

about the same time three ex-RAF Canberra P.R.9s were also acquired.

With the RAF's impending withdrawal at the end of 1971 Singapore, like the Gulf states, decided to provide its own air arm and this, known as the Singapore Air Defence Command, was established officially in September 1971; it was later renamed the Republic of Singapore Air Force. An initial order for 16 Hunter FGA.74s and F.R.74As (the latter with a camera nose) and four Hunter T.75 trainers was placed, and a further 22 FGA.74s and five two-seater T.75s were acquired later. These equip two strike squadrons based at the former RAF airfield of Tengah: No 140 (Osprey) Squadron, which has the four Hunter F.R.74As on strength, and No 141 (Merlin) Squadron, which between them now have 27 FGA.74s and four T.75s in service, as well as the F.R.74As. The Hunters are now equipped to carry AIM–9J Sidewinder missiles, and they are due for early replacement by A–4S Skyhawks.

Refurbishing the Hunter

Although some Hunter F.6s for export, such as the ones initially supplied to Iraq, Jordan and the Lebanon, and the first 12 aircraft of both the Swiss and Indian Air Forces orders, were supplied from RAF stocks with the minimum of modification, from 1964 onwards a growing business began to develop in the supply of Hunters refurbished and updated to the basic FGA.9 standard for resale to foreign air forces. These were mostly surplus Dutch and Belgian Hunter F.6s, with surplus RAF ones and also some F.4s and T.7s, and they were much more extensively rebuilt and updated than the original F.6s supplied from RAF stocks. The first surplus Hunters acquired by Hawker for refurbishing were a batch of 32 Belgian Air Force F.6s, all but one of which were flown in to Dunsfold by Hawker test pilots during the latter part of 1962 and early

1963, receiving the Hawker Class B registrations (applied to all Hunters destined for refurbishing) G–9–70 to G–9–101; the registrations G–9–70 to G–9–96 had previously been allotted to some of the Hunter F.50s built at Squires Gate for Sweden.

The next batch of surplus Hunters to arrive at Dunsfold were 21 Dutch Air Force F.6s and a T.7, delivered between February and April 1964; Dutch pilots flew in the serviceable F.6s and the remainder arrived by road. These aircraft had very nearly been used by the Dutch for fire-fighting experiments at Deelen air force base, but just in time Hawkers realised that these Hunters were still very saleable and acquired them, giving the Dutch 18 surplus Royal Navy Sea Fury F.B.11s for their fire-fighting trials in part exchange. The Dutch F.6s were registered G–9–165 to G–9–185 and the T.7, N–317, became G–9–164; it was followed by four more Dutch T.7s early in 1965, which became G–9–191 to G–9–194. A second batch of 64 ex-Belgian Hunter F.6s were flown into Dunsfold by Belgian Air Force pilots during late 1964 and early 1965, these becoming G–9–102 to G–9–163, plus G–9–186 and G–9–187. Of these last two, '–187 was the first Belgian-built F.6 and '–186, already partly converted to a ground-instructional airframe by the Belgians, went by road to the Hawker Apprentices Training School at Kingston. First deliveries of refurbished Hunters began late in 1964 when 18 from the first ex-Belgian batch were delivered to the Iraqi Air Force as Hunter F.59s, and four to Kuwait as F.57s, a further 26 Hunter F.59s for Iraq from the second Belgian batch following during 1965-66.

Later surplus RAF F.6s joined the Belgian and Dutch ones for refurbishing and resale, and whereas in 1957-58 the price of a brand new Hunter F.6 delivered to a Maintenance Unit was stated on the invoice (which came with those F.6s ordered under the Mutual

41

Defence Aid Programme) as about £90,000, by the early 1970s the price of a newly refurbished Hunter was upwards of £250,000. Indeed, depending on the avionics fit and the number of aircraft refurbished for a particular air force, refurbished Hunters could cost up to £500,000 apiece, but for this the customer got a virtually zero fatigue life aircraft, with up to 3,000 hours of combat life ahead of it, at a fraction of the cost of a factory-new modern equivalent type. In many cases the refurbishing included the fitting of new bottom main spar booms, these being kept in production for attachment to spare wings held in store; a new cockpit canopy, manufactured at the former Folland plant at Hamble, Hampshire, was often fitted and flying controls were brought up to the latest modification standard. A number of F.6s were converted into trainers by fitting a T.7-type two-seater nose, while at least one trainer was converted into a single-seater. Extensive reskinning of the fuselage and wings was sometimes undertaken, and the firm's stress office kept comprehensive records of each individual Hunter's service life to assess the degree of rebuilding that might be necessary.

On arrival for refurbishing, usually at Dunsfold but sometimes at the former Armstrong Whitworth airfield at Bitteswell, Hunters were made safe, disarmed and defuelled, and a receipt check was carried out along with a preliminary survey. The aircraft was dismantled into its major components, the fuselage being split into its three sections. Rear fuselages and wings went to Bitteswell, where major wing jigs were held, tail surfaces and cockpit canopies went to the ex-Folland plant at Hamble, and Avon engines were returned to Rolls-Royce for reconditioning and overhaul, each Avon usually being returned to its 'parent' aircraft, or if this was not possible, replaced by a stock Avon held by Rolls. The preliminary survey, carried out by the inspection department, recorded the aircraft's state and the work necessary to bring it up to a 're-delivery condition'. Each airframe part was then classified under one of three major headings: 'discard and replace', 'repair' or 'modify'. Design work went ahead on such things as new avionics and instruments fits specified by the customer, and the sort of details necessary to turn, for instance, an ex-Dutch F.6 into a T.79 trainer for Qatar, or an ex-Belgian F.6 into an F.56A for India.

On arrival at the appropriate factory, the dismantled Hunter's airframe sections were stripped of all pipes and most cables, while all proprietary parts such as hydraulics, pneumatics, oxygen systems and the like, were removed and returned to their manufacturers for reconditioning. Fuselage and wing skins were removed and replaced where necessary, and on later refurbished aircraft the underwing surface around the undercarriage pivot point was reskinned as a matter of course. A number of Hunter F.4s were refitted with the Avon 203 turbojet of the F.6, and since this Avon variant was of larger diameter than the Avon 113 or 122 of the F.4 what seemed at first to be the insoluble problem of fitting it into the F.4 was solved by a major rebuild of the engine bay. Using F.6-type vertical frames, this was rebuilt from aft of the main spar (frame 25) back to a modified frame 40a which formed the transport joint and engine attachment point; at the rear spar station frame 32 was rebuilt *in situ*. During rebuilding the fuel tank around the jet pipe, which did not feature in the F.4, was fitted. At first the F.4 was not refurbished because its wing, with only two 'stores' pylons, could not carry the heavier attack loads of the F.6 and FGA.9; for the same reason, the 16 ex-Danish Hunter F.51s returned to Dunsfold in 1976 were not refurbished. Altogether 302 Hunter fighters and 52 trainers were refurbished and updated for resale to more than a dozen air forces, although by 1976-77 the supply of surplus Hunters had largely dried up, and there was a shortage of suitable Avon engines.

J–4101, seen here, formerly XG127 and G–9–294, was the first of 52 refurbished Hunter F.58As supplied to the Swiss Air Force from 1972 to 1976. These now have Saab BT9K bombing computers and Sidewinder air-to-air missiles, and can also carry the Hughes AGM–65 Maverick air-to-ground missile.

The Hunter Trainers

Such was the retarding effect of the ill-judged 1957 Defence White Paper on Hunter development that the only new version after the F.6 to go into production, and this only because of Sir Sydney Camm's persistence, was the Hunter T.7 two-seater trainer; all subsequent variants were conversions of Hunter F.4s or F.6s. Even so, only 45 T.7s were ordered for the RAF, and had a trainer variant been ordered into production earlier, more would doubtless have been sold. Design work on a two-seat trainer had begun as a private venture in 1953, and both tandem-seat and side-by-side cockpit layouts were evaluated, the choice between the two being guided by the expert opinions of instructors and staffs of the Central Flying School and the Day Fighter Leaders' School of the Central Fighter Establishment. By mid-1953 the side-by-side arrangement had been chosen largely because it was easier to demonstrate the controls to a pupil, and weapon sighting and instrument flying instruction would be easier. Originally the mock-up of the two-seater cockpit hood had featured a separate bulge over each pilot, but for ease of production this double bulge was smoothed out to give a pair of transparent panels in a massive frame, the entire hood being hinged to open upwards and backwards electrically. In this form the Hawker P.1101, as the trainer was known, met Specification T.157D issued in 1954, and two prototypes were ordered.

The first of these, XJ615, made its maiden flight on 8 July 1955 and was based on the Hunter F.4, with a 'small bore' Avon 122 engine of 7,500-lb (3,400-kg) s.t. and two 30-mm Aden cannon semi-recessed in blisters and firing

through blast tubes on either side of the nosewheel. The slightly wider forward fuselage was 3 ft (1.02 m) longer than the single-seat FGA.9's, and the instructor and pupil had fully duplicated flying controls and gunsights, as well as Martin-Baker Mk 4 lightweight ejector seats. Tests on the ejection configuration of these seats were carried out on the Hunter T.7 second prototype XJ627, using a screen between the two pilots, the aircraft being loaned to Martin-Baker for these trials. In 1956 a G.Q. tail-braking parachute was fitted to the first prototype XJ615 after one had been tried earlier on the F.4 WT780; the braking parachute was housed in a 'pen nib' fairing over the jet pipe. The second prototype, XJ627, first flew on 17 November 1956; this was based on the Hunter F.6 and had a 10,000-lb (4,540-kg) s.t. Avon 203 engine, a larger cockpit hood fairing, a slightly different windscreen shape and only one 30-mm Aden in a fairing under the starboard side of the fuselage. XJ627 had the 'dog tooth' wing leading edge extensions, and an anti-spin parachute was later fitted.

Flight tests with XJ615 revealed a troublesome snag: at speeds over about Mach 0.84 airflow instability around the cockpit hood and its fairing started to build up so that at Mach 0.88 the aircraft would commence snaking and pitching, and noise from the airflow increased sharply. First attempts to find a cure took the form of trials with vortex generators around the windscreen arch to stimulate the boundary layer so as to delay airflow separation; between 12 and 36 of these generators were fitted at different times. Also, the 30-mm Aden blisters were altered in shape temporarily or removed altogether so as to vary the fuselage cross-section just forward of the wings. Finally the fairing aft of the cockpit hood was enlarged, at first by degrees, and as the result of doing this proved encouraging the entire

The Hunter T.7 prototype XJ615 in its original form before the fairing aft of the cockpit was enlarged.

fairing was re-contoured according to the then still new Area Rule theory. The now familiar hump-backed fairing aft of the hood provided the remedy, and by mid-1956 about 24 different cockpit hood configurations had been tried and flown on XJ615, and metal hoods were finally used on the prototype because they were cheaper. Details of the revised hood and fairing were later forwarded by Hawker to English Electric to help them with the design of the Lightning T.4, the side-by-side trainer version of the Lightning F.1A.

Production Hunter T.7s for the RAF were based on the first prototype XJ615, with the Avon 122 engine and one starboard-mounted Aden gun as on the second prototype XJ627. Originally 65 T.7s for the RAF were ordered, but ten of these (to have been XM117-XM126) were diverted to the Royal Netherlands Air Force, and a further ten to the Royal Navy as Hunter T.8s; the Dutch later ordered a further ten T.7s. The T.7s were to have been built at Squires Gate, but with the ending of Hunter production they were built at Kingston, as were the ten Royal Navy T.8s. The first production T.7, XL563, made its maiden flight on 11 October 1957, and RAF T.7s were serialled XL563-XL579, XL583, XL586, XL587, XL591-7, XL600, XL601, XL605 and XL609-XL623. One reason why more T.7s were not built was that Hunter F.4s could be converted into T.7s, the different nose sections being interchangeable forward of the front transport joint, but in the end only six F.4s were converted to T.7s in 1958-59, five by Armstrong Whitworth and one, XF310 which had carried out trials of the Fireflash missile, by Hawker. Thirty-one F.4s were also converted to T.8s for the Royal Navy. Hunter T.7s first entered service with No 229 OCU at Chivenor, near Barnstaple, in mid-1958, and some also went to the Central Fighter Establishment; T.7s were later issued to squadrons in Fighter Command and in Germany for use in instrument flight check-outs. The T.7 was originally to have replaced the Vampire T.11 in the Advanced Flying Schools, but the latter type survived until the Advanced Flying Schools were disbanded or they were replaced by Jet Provosts. Three Hunter T.7s served with the Weapons Training Squadron at Sylt, and some others were based at RAF Khormaksar in Aden.

Following the loss early on of a Hunter T.7 in an inverted spin, a very thorough test programme to investigate the T.7's spinning behaviour was put in hand under A.W. 'Bill' Bedford. This culminated triumphantly at the 1959 and 1960 SBAC Shows when Bedford in the Hunter T.66A demonstrator G–APUX did a 12-turn spin from 15,000 ft (4,572 m), the course of the spin being made visible to the crowds by the injection of diesel oil into the jet efflux to produce white smoke. G–APUX was produced by the rebuilding of a badly damaged Belgian Air Force Hunter F.6, serial IF.19, which had made a wheel-up forced landing; this was fitted at Kingston with the two-seater forward fuselage of an Indian Air Force T.66, serial BS369, and the complete aircraft was erected at Dunsfold in July 1959. It had two Aden cannon and a 10,050-lb (4,563-kg) s.t. Avon 207C engine, and differed from other T.7s in having a Dunlop

nosewheel brake with Maxaret anti-skid device to bring the landing run down to below 1,500 ft (460 m); a radio compass was also fitted but this and the nosewheel brake were later removed.

Bill Bedford made a series of flights in G–APUX and had it so perfectly adjusted and trimmed that he said it was 'the sweetest Hunter I have ever had the pleasure to fly'. In 1960 it was fitted with two extra-large 350-Imp gal (1,591-litres) ferry drop tanks, made by inserting 3-ft (1.02-m) sections into 230-Imp gal (1,045-litres) drop tanks. The 350-Imp gal tanks now had a lateral bracing strut to the wing, and were stressed to take 7g loads for use on ground-attack missions, although these big tanks were never fitted on production Hunters. G–APUX was later used for trials at Farnborough of the Rank Cintel Peep head-up instrumentation, and in May 1963 it was leased to the Iraqi Air Force with the serial '567' (a serial also used by a Hunter T.69 for Iraq) pending delivery of two Hunter T.69s to Iraq. It returned from lease to Iraq after a year and then went on loan for a period to both the Lebanese Air Force and Jordan's air force. G–APUX returned to Dunsfold from these spells of foreign service on 18 December 1965 and later became G–9–232 before being sold in August 1967 as J–718 to the Fuerza Aerea de Chile as one of four Hunter T.72s acquired by them. Among these was the second prototype T.7 XJ627, which became G–9–296 and then J–721.

The first trainers to be exported were two Hunter T.53s to the Royal Danish Air Force in 1958, serialled ET–271 and ET–272; these were very similar to the RAF's T.7 and were later supplemented by two ex-RAF T.7s, which became ET–273 and ET–274. After being withdrawn from service and in open store for some time all four were shipped back to Hatfield via Harwich at the

beginning of 1976, being given the Class B registrations G–9–429 to G–9–432 respectively. Sixteen Danish Hunter F.51s made surplus by the disbandment of the final flight of *Eskadrille* 724 on 31 March 1974 were likewise returned to Dunsfold at the same time. One Hunter T.62 was delivered to the Fuerza Aérea del Peru late in 1959, and was serialled 681; like the Danish and Dutch Hunter trainers it had the 'small bore' Avon 122 engine.

Of the 20 Hunter T.7s acquired by the Dutch Air Force (they did not have an export mark number) ten, serialled N–311 to N–320, were diverted from the RAF order and were to have been XM117-XM126; the other ten were serialled N–301 to N–310. One of these T.7s, N–320, was used to carry a Dutch senior staff observer on operational interception sorties to ensure that no guns were fired in anger by other Dutch aircraft on the sortie. Most of the Dutch T.7s were returned to Hawker from 1964-65 for refurbishing and resale but one, N–320, was registered PH–NLH to the National Lucht en Ruimtevaartlaboratorium (National Air and Space Research Centre). It was delivered in civil guise to Amsterdam's Schiphol Airport on 28 May 1964, painted bright blue with a white fuselage top and fin and rudder, and it was used for various research jobs such as cockpit pressurisation tests.

First customer to order the Hunter trainer with the 'big bore' Avon 203 of 10,000 lb (4,540 kg) s.t. was the Indian Air Force, which ordered 16 Hunter T.66s in 1957 and a further six later on; these were based on the F.6 and had two 30-mm Adens and a tail-braking parachute. Deliveries of these began in 1959 and finished in February 1961, and a further 12 Hunter T.66Ds converted and refurbished from ex-Dutch F.6s were delivered from July to September 1967; and at least one more T.66D was acquired about six years later. These 12 were serialled S–570 to

Above: An early trainer export was the sole Hunter T.62 '681' for the Fuerza Aerea del Peru; this was converted from Hunter F.4 WT706 and was delivered late in 1959.

Right: The cockpit and instrument panel of the Hunter T.7.

Below: Hunter T.66A demonstrator G–APUX in Iraqi Air Force markings with the serial 567 in white Arabic letters on the rear fuselage. After being leased to Iraq for a year from May 1963, it was also loaned to the air forces of Lebanon and Jordan, and was finally sold to the Fuerza Aerea de Chile as J–718 in August 1967.

S–581, and were among the first of a number of single-seater Hunters refurbished as trainers. The Indian T.66s and T.66Ds served with Nos 7, 14, 17, 20 and 27 Squadrons based at Ambala and Poona.

King Hussein of Jordan had flown one of the Indian T.66s at Dunsfold while on a visit to this country and this led to two Hunter T.66Bs being supplied to the Royal Jordanian Air Force, and a third later. The first of these, serialled 714, was delivered in July 1960 and the two others, refurbished from ex-Dutch F.6s, were 716 and 800; these differed from the Indian T.66s in having an Avon 207 engine instead of the Avon 203. In 1975 Jordan disposed of 31 Hunter FGA.73As and 73Bs to the Sultan of Oman's Air Force, along with the T.66Bs 716 and 800, and these now equipped No 6 Squadron at Thumrayt. The T.66Bs 716 and 800 were given the Omani serials 802 and 801 respectively. The Royal Saudi Air Force had acquired two Hunter T.7s, 70–616 (ex- G–9–215 and XL620) and 70-617 (ex- G–9–

214 and XL605) in May and June 1966 to provide jet experience for Saudi pilots pending delivery of their Lightning F.53s and T.55s. These T.7s were later sold to the Royal Jordanian Air Force and in 1972 were returned to the UK with their old RAF serials. They were modified back to T.7 standard and given new RAF serials, XL620 becoming XX466 and XL605 becoming XX467, the former going to No 229 OCU at Chivenor. Both later served with Nos 1 and 2 TWU.

The Force Aérienne Libanaise acquired two Hunter T.66s which, with single-seat Hunters, equipped one day-fighter squadron and were used in the ground-attack role. The T.66s were still in service in 1983 although, like the other Lebanese Hunters, they have not flown a great deal in the civil war. As related earlier, the Iraqi Air Force leased the T.66A demonstrator G–APUX in May 1963 for a year pending the delivery of the two Hunter T.69s on order. Three more T.69s were later acquired by Iraq, and the T.69s are believed to be still in service. The Kuwaiti Air

Four Dutch Air Force Hunter T.7s in formation; of these, N–307 later became G–BOOM and N–304 went to the Singapore Air Defence Command as Hunter T.75 '504'.

Force ordered two factory-new Hunter T.67 trainers which, like the Jordanian T.66Bs, had the Avon 207 engine and these T.67s left Dunsfold on their delivery flight to Kuwait on 25 February 1965. Some years later three more T.67s refurbished from F.6s were acquired and the T.67s and F.57s equipped one ground-attack squadron. The T.67s have now been withdrawn following re-equipment with A–4KU Skyhawks for the strike role, and two of them were disposed of to the Sultan of Oman's Air Force with the serials 803 and 804; they form part of the Omani No 6 Squadron's Hunter strength.

Two Hunter T.77s serialled 711 and 712 were supplied to the Abu Dhabi Defence Force Air Wing, these being the refurbished ex-Dutch Air Force T.7s N–312 and N–301 respectively, with the Class B registrations G–9–288 and G–9–

289. They later served with the United Emirates Air Force when this was created and, like the single-seat Hunters, were based on permanent detachment in Sharjah. After being replaced by Hawk T.61s and T.63s, they were passed on in 1983 to the Somali Aeronautical Corps. One Hunter T.79 serialled QA–12 was supplied to the Qatar Emiri Air Force, this being the refurbished ex-Dutch F.6 N–222 which had the Class B registration G–9–284. The T.79 supplemented three Hunter FGA.78s based at Doha, and is still in service. One Hunter T.80 was supplied to the Kenya Air Force in July 1974.

The Swiss Air Force had not ordered the Hunter trainer with its initial order for 100 Hunter F.58s in 1958, but when more refurbished Hunter F.58As were acquired from 1972 the opportunity was taken to add eight Hunter T.68 trainers to the Swiss inventory, these being serialled J–4201 to J–4208. As related in a previous chapter, the final assembly of these refurbished F.58As and T.68s, and the application of Swiss Air Force modifications to them, was undertaken by the Swiss Federal Aircraft Factory at its Emmen works. Some T.68s have now been equipped for the ECM role. As related earlier, the Fuerza Aerea de Chile acquired four Hunter T.72s from refurbished stocks, and these included the T.66A demonstrator

G–APUX, which became J–718, and the second prototype T.7 XJ627, which became J–721. The Singapore Air Defence Command ordered four Hunter T.75 trainers initially after its formation in 1971, and acquired five more T.75s later. The four surviving T.75s are now on the strength of the two Tengah-based strike squadrons, No 140 (Osprey) Squadron and No 141 (Merlin) Squadron, of what is now the Republic of Singapore Air Force.

Meanwhile in RAF service Hunter T.7s joined No 4 Flying Training School at Valley in Anglesey in January 1967, supplementing the Gnat T.1s already there; late in 1979 some T.7s of this unit joined No 237 OCU at Honington in Suffolk, which also operated Hawk T.1s. Hunter T.7s continued to serve with No 229 OCU at Chivenor, this moving to Brawdy late in 1974 and taking its Hunters with it to become No 1 Tactical Weapons Unit. In 1978 No 2 Tactical Weapons Unit at Lossiemouth was formed from No 1 TWU, and by 1980 the former had nine T.7s on strength and No 1 TWU had seven. Among No 2 TWU's aircraft in 1980 was the veteran XF310, coded 01, built as an F.4 and which had carried out the Fireflash missile trials a quarter of a century before. No 2 TWU's T.7s were replaced by the Hawk T.1, which was also the foremost type with No 1 TWU, but the latter still had

nine T.7s at the beginning of 1983. Following the introduction of the TACAN navaid to Royal Navy Hunter T.8s, some RAF T.7s were also fitted with it, this variant being designated T.7A. Some more T.7s were modified into Hunter T.7Ds by fitting much of the Buccaneer S.2's internal instrumentation for training purposes. They are used by the RAF's Buccaneer squadrons, Nos 12 and 208 at Honington, Suffolk, and Nos 15 and 16 at Laarbruch, Germany, to provide instrument flying training and checkouts, and weapons and tactical handling checks for front-line pilots, as there is no dual control trainer variant of the Buccaneer.

The sole Hunter T.12 XE531, painted green and cream, was converted from an F.6 into a two-seater, and was used extensively to test the Specto Avionics' head-up instrument display intended for use with the TSR.2 and its terrain-following radar. Much of the equipment associated with this was installed in one vacated gun bay; there was an empty gun blister on the starboard side. A large vertically-mounted survey camera was fitted in the nose, and XE531 also had a tail-braking parachute and an Avon 207

J-4201 seen here was the first of eight Hunter T.68s for the Swiss Air Force, and was formerly F.4 WV332, 7673M and G-9–406. It first flew as a T.68 in Switzerland in May 1975 and this variant has the standard Avon 207 engine.

Hunter T.8 XL580 in its very attractive navy-blue-and-white colour scheme was used as an 'admiral's barge' by the Flag Officer Flying Training at RNAS Yeovilton.

engine. After the TSR.2's cancellation in 1965 XE531 continued to serve as one of the main avionics test beds at RAE Farnborough, but crashed while taking off there on 17 March 1982, injuring one of the two pilots. Hunter T.7 WV253:24 was used by the Empire Test Pilots' School in an attractive scarlet and white colour scheme, and had an instrumentation boom in the nose; the prototype T.7s XJ615 and XJ627 also served for a time with the ETPS. Another research Hunter was used to investigate the problems of low-level navigation at night.

The Navy's Hunters

By the late 1950s the Fleet Air Arm needed a jet trainer of higher performance than the Sea Vampire T.22s and Meteor T.7s it then had in service, and so the Hunter T.8 was produced as the Navy's version of the T.7; the first T.8 WW664, a converted F.4, first flew in this form on 3 March 1958. The T.8 differed from the T.7 only in having naval radio, slightly different instrumentation and an arrestor hook under the rear fuselage for use with naval airfield emergency arrestor gear, but the hook and its attachment were not stressed for deck landings which, in fact, were never undertaken by the Hunter. Ten Hunter T.8s were built at Kingston, being diverted

from the RAF's order for T.7s; these were XL580-2, XL584, XL585, XL598, XL599 and XL602-4. A further 18 initially were converted from F.4s; these all had the 'small bore' Avon 122 engine like the T.7, and equipped Nos 738, 759 and 764 Squadrons at Yeovilton in Somerset and Lossiemouth in Morayshire. T.8s first entered Naval service with No 764 Squadron at RNAS Lossiemouth in July 1958. At first the T.8s were used for conversion training but they were later fitted with the wiring and circuitry to enable them to fire salvoes of 2-in (50.8-mm) rocket projectiles. Later provision was made for them to carry the Martin AGM–12 Bullpup air-to-surface missile which could also be fitted to Buccaneers and Sea Vixens.

Following the introduction of TACAN (tactical air navigation) to Fleet Air Arm aircraft, this being a UHF (ultra high frequency) navaid giving bearing/distance of an aircraft from an interrogated ground station, Hunter T.8s were modified to incorporate it. This led to the Aden cannon and the radar-ranging gunsight in the extreme nose being removed. During 1963-64 13 more F.4s were converted to this standard as T.8Bs and T.8Cs, with TACAN and an OR.946 instrument display; the T.8B had a full TACAN installation and the T.8C was an interim variant until it could be brought up to the full T.8B standard. From 1978 two Hunter T.8Cs, XL602

and XL603, were used to test the multi-mode Ferranti Blue Fox radar of the Sea Harrier FRS.1, its avionics and Smiths head-up display; with this they were redesignated T.8Ms, a third T.8C, XL580, being later modified to this standard. The T.8Ms afterwards went to RNAS Yeovilton for use as Sea Harrier radar and systems trainers for No 899 Squadron; with this unit XL580 was coded 719 and XL603 was coded 720. XL580 had previously served the Flag Officer Flying Training, Rear Admiral Gick, at Yeovilton as an 'admiral's barge', being finished in a very attractive navy blue and white colour scheme. It was succeeded by a second T.8, XL584, in this role of personal transport and this in turn was succeeded by a third T.8, XE665, converted from an F.6.

The second version of the Hunter to be used by the Fleet Air Arm was a conversion of the F.4 for ground-attack training known as the Hunter GA.11, this being a single-seater with the Avon 122 engine. The Aden cannon and radar-ranging gunsight in the nose were removed, but comprehensive wiring and circuitry were fitted for a variety of underwing weapon loads, ranging from 1,000-lb (454-kg) bombs to the Martin AGM-12B Bullpup-A air-to-surface missile, of which one was carried under each wing. The Bullpup was controlled in flight by the pilot, who used a hand-switch to transmit radio command signals to the missile. The GA.11 also had an arrestor hook under the rear fuselage for use with airfield emergency arrestor gear, but not for deck landings, and TACAN equipment was fitted, as well as the 'dog tooth' wing leading edge extensions of the Hunter F.6. For PR sorties a nose with three cameras, similar to the Hunter F.R.10's, could be fitted in place of the standard 'plain' nose, the GA.11 sometimes being known as the P.R.11 in this form. The first GA.11 first flew on 24 January 1962, and 40 F.4s were converted to GA.11s, serving with Nos 738, 759 and 764 Squadrons.

The Royal Navy acquired its GA.11s very cheaply at about £33,000 each, and the first were delivered in June 1962 to No 738 Squadron based at Lossiemouth and Brawdy; this had 12 GA.11s and six T.8s on charge by the end of 1962. In 1967 a Fleet Air Arm aerobatic team of three GA.11s and a T.8 was formed, led by Lieutenant Commander Chris Comins.

In 1969 the Hunter GA.11 began to re-equip the Fleet Requirements Unit (FRU) operated under contract by Airwork Ltd at Hurn Airport, Bournemouth, Dorset, the first two GA.11s arriving to replace Scimitars in March that year. Now known as the Fleet Requirements and Air Direction Unit (FRADU) and based at Yeovilton, this provides for ships of the Royal Navy (and sometimes foreign warships) anti-ship missile simulation sorties, radio and radar calibration, gunnery tracking support and target towing, Hunter GA.11s and T.8Cs being used for the first three roles and Canberra T.T.18s for the last. The Unit had 14 GA.11s and eight T.8Cs on strength by 1984. The Hunters and Canberras were maintained and flown by Airwork personnel, and the Unit has a small number of Royal Navy staff to co-ordinate the requirements of FRADU's 'customers'.

Both GA.11s and T.8Cs are now fitted with a powerful Harley light in the nose to aid visual acquisition and tracking by gun crews, and this light enables a Hunter to be seen in favourable conditions at ranges of up to 10 miles (16.1 km). The Unit's Canberra T.22s fitted with Blue Parrot radar in the nose are also used for anti-ship missile simulation and, with one or two Hunters formating on the wing tip of one of these Canberras to simulate air-to-surface missiles, a missile attack from an enemy bomber can be simulated. The Hunters also fly practice interception sorties for the benefit of trainee Fighter Controllers of the Royal Navy's Direction Officers School, known as 'D' School, at Yeovilton. The FRADU used to have an aerobatic team of four GA.11s known as the 'Blue Herons', formed in July 1975, but

this had to be disbanded a few years ago because of the pressure of the Unit's other commitments; it was unusual in being the world's first military jet aerobatic team to be flown by civilian pilots, the GA.11s used being WT806, WV382, WW654 and XF977. At the end of 1983 Flight Refuelling (Services) Ltd were awarded a Ministry of Defence contract to operate the FRADU in place of Airwork, and are employing some 200 personnel on this contract.

Bottom: One of the three Hunter T.8Cs used to test the multi-mode Ferranti Blue Fox radar of the Sea Harrier FRS.1 plus its avionics and Smiths head-up display; in this form they are redesignated as T.8Ms.

Below: Hunter GA.11 WV258:862, one of 40 F.4s converted to this mark, serves with the Fleet Requirements and Air Direction Unit (FRADU) providing gunnery and target practice for ships of the Royal Navy.

The Hunter FGA.9 and F.R.10

In 1958 trials began to select the RAF's future ground-attack fighter for use in the Middle East and tropical climates, to replace the now elderly Venom F.B.1s and F.B.4s previously used in these regions. This selection process was held under the general direction of the Central Fighter Establishment and the A & AEE, and involved assessment of the Folland Gnat F.1, the Jet Provost and the Hunter F.6, the latter being chosen for trials in Aden with the Air Fighting Development School (AFDS), two F.6s, XK150 and XK151, undergoing evaluation there. This led to the Hunter FGA.9, which differed from the F.6 in having the 10,150-lb (4,604-kg) s.t. Avon 207 engine instead of the Avon 203, some structural strengthening, a 10-ft 6-in (3.20-m) diameter ring-slot braking parachute over the jet pipe nozzle similar to the parachute fitted to Swiss and Indian Hunters, increased oxygen reserves for the pilot, a boosted air conditioning system, high-capacity main tyres and brakes and cutaway flaps to allow attachment of the big 230-Imp gal (1,045-litres) drop tanks on the inner pylons. The prototype FGA.9, XE617, first flew on 3 July 1959 and in all 120 Mk 9s were converted from F.6s. Pending delivery of the first FGA.9s a stop-gap variant known as the Mk 6/Interim Mk 9 was produced by converting F.6s at RAF Maintenance Units; this variant featured only the modifications associated with the 230-Imp gal (1,045-litres) drop tanks, which were used for ferrying and overseas reinforcement only, and did not have the Avon 207 or tail-braking parachute. By 1961 almost all of this interim variant had been brought up to full FGA.9

standard, and some years later the designation Hunter F.6A was applied to F.6s of No 1 Tactical Weapons Unit brought up to FGA.9 standard.

First squadron to convert to the Hunter FGA.9 was No 8 at Khormaksar, Aden, in January 1960; the first Mk 9s were delivered to them in October 1959 and these were frequently in action against incursions from the Yemeni forces, who were backed by Egypt's Colonel Nasser, across the border into the Aden Protectorate, which in 1962 became part of the South Arabian Federation. No 8 Squadron also participated when British troops were sent to Kuwait in July 1961 to resist an Iraqi claim on that country. Following Britain's withdrawal from Aden No 8 Squadron moved to Muharraq on Bahrain in September 1967 as part of our military presence in the Gulf, and in September 1971 a further move was made to Sharjah before No 8 was disbanded on 15 December that year. No 208 Squadron at Stradishall, Suffolk, converted to FGA.9s in March 1960, replacing its Venom F.B.4s, and moved to Aden in December 1961, a further move to Muharraq on Bahrain being made in June 1964; here the squadron remained until disbanded on 10 September 1971. No 43 Squadron also introduced FGA.9s in 1960 at its Leuchars base and moved to Nicosia in Cyprus in June 1961; it went to Aden in March 1963 to provide air support for the Army, and stayed there until disbanded on 14 October 1967, just after the British withdrawal from Aden. Two other Hunter FGA.9 units served in the Far East; No 20 Squadron at Tengah, Singapore, was based here until it was disbanded on 13 February 1970, after being reformed at Tengah with FGA.9s on 3 July 1961; it did a spell on detachment to Thailand from May to November 1962 as part of a SEATO deployment to counter Communist military activities in the Thai/Laos border regions. No 28 Squadron,

which had been based at Hong Kong since May 1949, received its first Hunter FGA.9s in May 1962 to replace Venom F.B.4s, and it flew the Mk 9s until disbanding on 2 January 1967.

The two most important home-based FGA.9 units were No 1 Squadron and No 54 Squadron, both of which were based at Stradishall in Suffolk and received their Mk 9s in March 1960, replacing F.6s. These two units later formed the ground-attack support wing of Transport Command's No 38 Group, forming part of a tactical Army support force under this Group consisting, initially, of Hastings C.1As and C.2s and Beverley C.1s for the main tactical transport role, Pioneers and Twin Pioneers for light transport and Belvedere, Whirlwind and Wessex helicopters. Both No 1 and No 54 moved to Waterbeach, Cambridgeshire, in November 1961 and to West Raynham in Norfolk in August 1963. In July 1969 No 1 moved to Wittering in Northamptonshire to convert to the Harrier GR.1, so becoming the world's first operational VTOL fighter squadron. No 54 was scheduled to follow it in equipping with Harriers, but instead disbanded on 1 September 1969, its remaining FGA.9s and pilots being transferred to No 4 Squadron as the UK echelon of this unit, which was based at Gutersloh in Germany and had Hunter F.R.10s. As the UK echelon of No 4 Squadron, this remnant of No 54 remained at West Raynham until March 1970 when it moved to Wittering to convert to Harrier GR.1s, and with these it became No 4 Squadron on 28 May that year, the remainder of No 4 at Gutersloh being disbanded. Also at West Raynham was No 45 Squadron, reformed on 1 August 1972 with Hunter FGA.9s after being disbanded as a Canberra B.2 unit two years before; this moved to Wittering in September 1972 and used its Mk 9s for ground-attack training until disbanding again on 4 June 1976. Reformed from No 45 Squadron at Wittering exactly a year after that unit had restarted with Hunters, No 58 Squadron used its FGA.9s to provide operational strike and continuation training for Jaguar pilots until it disbanded on the same date as No 45; both squadrons were part of No 38 Group.

After its service with the squadrons, the Hunter FGA.9 continued to fly with No 1 Tactical Weapons Unit at Brawdy, which had 22 of this mark in 1976, but following the formation of No 2 Tactical Weapons Unit at Lossiemouth two years later from No 1 TWU, some of the latter's Mk 9s went to No 2 TWU, which had 26 FGA.9s in 1980. Most of these were later returned to No 1 TWU at Brawdy, which in 1983 still had 16 FGA.9s in service, five of which were modified for target towing. No 2 TWU had been formed at Lossiemouth to relieve the congestion at Brawdy as increasing numbers of Hawk T.1s were delivered to No 1 TWU, and No 2 moved to Chivenor in Devon in 1980 following the arrival of two Buccaneer squadrons at Lossiemouth. No 1 TWU is organised into three 'shadow' squadrons, Nos 63, 79 and 234, which continue the memory of disbanded former Hunter units.

Meanwhile in December 1962 the first pair of Hunter FGA.9s to be exported left Dunsfold on delivery to the Royal Rhodesian Air Force, which had ordered 12, serialled RRAF116 to RRAF127. These were all refurbished from ex-RAF F.6s, and were finished in Fighter Command camouflage with the RAF-type roundels bearing three assegais on each red central disc. They equipped the RRAF's No 1 Squadron which, with No 2 Squadron and its Vampire F.B.9s and two Canberra B.2 squadrons, was based at Thornhill, Gwelo. After Rhodesia's Unilateral Declaration of Independence in November 1965 the UK placed an embargo on spares and the further supply of combat aircraft to the

Rhodesian Air Force (the 'Royal' prefix being dropped after UDI). But in spite of this the Air Force continued to fly, with little diminution of its strength, and in fact a number of light aircraft of several types were acquired after the UN sanctions ban for use in the COIN role, for casualty evacuation, forward air control and reconnaissance.

As the war against guerilla forces intensified in the 1970s, the Hunters took part in a number of air strikes on guerilla bases and camps in neighbouring Zambia and Mozambique, and also Botswana. Cut off by UN sanctions from spares and other supplies, the Rhodesians developed several of their own special weapons for air strikes. One of these was the Golf bomb, weighing about 1,000 lb

Above: A Hunter F.R.10 with a nose containing three cameras; just visible above the nosewheel door is the port for one of the oblique cameras.

Top: The first Hunter FGA.9 for the Royal Rhodesian Air Force, RRAF116, seen here just before its delivery in December 1962.

(454 kg), which had a tube or proboscis 3-ft (0.91-m) long protruding from the nose which struck the ground first, causing the bomb to detonate just above ground rather than in it for maximum anti-personnel effect. Two of these Golf bombs were carried by a Hunter and released in a 60° dive; one Golf was fitted with two plates which opened out during descent to retard its fall, so that it hit the ground a fraction of a

second after the other Golf, and in a slightly different position. The Hunters could carry a combination of Golfs and general purpose bombs on air strikes, and these proved to be very effective. Another weapon carried by the Hunter, but used only twice before anti-guerilla operations ceased, was a frangible casing holding 4,600 flechettes, which were similar to 6-in (152-mm) nails fitted with plastic tails; these were intended for use against guerilla encampments at night. Another Rhodesian-developed weapon was the Frantan (short for 'frangible tank') napalm bomb, which held 18 galls (81.8 litres) of napalm.

By 1978 there were still nine Hunter FGA.9s in service with No 1 Squadron, and the following year the country was renamed Zimbabwe-Rhodesia, later becoming Zimbabwe, the air arm becoming the Air Force of Zimbabwe – AFZ. Following President Robert Mugabe's victory in the general elections of early 1980, the process of integrating former guerilla units into the country's armed forces began. In 1981 the AFZ acquired four more

Hunter FGA.9s and a T.80 trainer from the Kenya Air Force, which had recently re-equipped with Northrop F–5Es and F–5Fs, and these made good the losses sustained in the long anti-guerilla campaign. On 25 July 1982 the AFZ suffered damage by sabotage when a bomb attack was made on aircraft parked at Thornhill air base, resulting in the loss of three Hunters, a brand-new Hawk T.54 (one of eight ordered) and a Reims/Cessna 337 Lynx light COIN aircraft, another eight aircraft being damaged. The motive for this attack and who was responsible remained obscure, although it led to the arrest and trial of several white AFZ officers, including the Chief of Operations and his deputy.

The Kenya Air Force took delivery of five Hunter FGA.9s and a T.80 trainer in July 1974 to form

an interceptor and strike squadron based at Nanyuki, supplementing an attack/trainer squadron with five BAC Strikemaster Mk 87s. The five remaining Hunters were withdrawn from use in 1980 and were later sold to Zimbabwe. As related in a previous chapter, many Hunter F.6s were refurbished and updated to FGA.9 standard for resale to foreign air forces, but two more countries acquired ex-RAF FGA.9s: the Force Aérienne Libanaise took delivery of five to supplement their original Hunter F.6s, and the Fuerza Aérea de Chile acquired a further seven FGA.9s from No 1 TWU at Brawdy in July 1982, these being brought up to FGA.71 standard to make up attrition and losses among the 30 of this mark delivered in batches since 1967.

The Hunter F.R.10 was a tactical reconnaissance version of the FGA.9 retaining all the features of that mark, such as the Avon 207 and braking parachute, but with one forward-facing and two oblique cameras in the nose, the four Aden cannons being retained. Like the Mk 9, the F.R.10 was produced by conversions of existing F.6s, 30 of these being made, and the prototype F.R.10, XF429, made its first flight on 7 November 1958, being converted from an Armstrong Whitworth-built F.6. The camera nose increased the overall length to 46 ft 1½ in (14.06 m), and the F.R.10 could carry the same drop tanks and underwing 'stores' as the FGA.9. Hunter F.R.10s replaced Swift F.R.5s in the only two units to have the latter type, Nos 2 and 79 Squadrons based in Germany with the 2nd Tactical Air Force. No 2 received its first F.R.10s in March 1961 at Jever, moving to Gutersloh in September that year, and the F.R.10s continued in service with No 2 for ten years, being replaced by Phantom FGR.2s. No 79 received its F.R.10s in December 1960 at Gutersloh but was renumbered 4 Squadron on 1 January 1961,

continuing to fly its Mk 10s until May 1970. As related earlier, the FGA.9s of the disbanded No 54 Squadron joined No 4 at West Raynham as its UK echelon, this part later converting to Harrier GR.1s at Wittering and becoming the new No 4 Squadron on 28 May 1970, the Gutersloh-based F.R.10s being disbanded. Another unit to operate Mk 9 and 10 versions of the Hunter was No 8 Squadron at Khormaksar, Aden, whose Meteor F.R.9s that equipped C Flight were replaced by Hunter F.R.10s in April 1961, the rest of the squadron, which had Venom F.B.4s, having re-equipped with Hunter FGA.9s in January 1960. The reconnaissance flight of F.R.10s became No 1417 (Fighter-reconnaissance) Flight in May 1963, and returned to No 8 in September 1967 when the squadron moved to Bahrain after Britain's withdrawal from Aden; the F.R.10s continued to serve until the squadron disbanded in December 1971, three months after moving to Sharjah.

Four Hunter F.R.10s were later supplied to the Iraqi Air Force to supplement its F.6s and F.59s, and one ex-RAF F.R.10, XF426, later went to the Royal Jordanian Air Force with the serial 853. This was later acquired by the Sultan of Oman's Air Force in 1975 along with 31 Hunter FGA.73As and 73Bs also acquired from Jordan; this F.R.10 retains the serial 853 in Omani service. Earlier one of the 12 Hunter F.6s supplied to Jordan, serial 712, was modified to F.R.6 standard with three cameras in the nose; this made it very similar to the F.R.10 but it did not have the tail-braking parachute, although it did have the 230-Imp gal (1,045-litre) drop tanks. Among the many Hunter F.6s refurbished and updated to FGA.9 standard for resale to foreign air forces, a few were fitted with camera noses similar to the F.R.10; these included three Hunter F.R.71As for the Fuerza Aerea de Chile, four F.R.74As for the Republic of Singapore Air Force, where they serve with No 140 (Osprey) Squadron, and a few F.R.76As for the Abu Dhabi Defence Force Air Wing, which later became part of the United Emirates Air Force.

The FGA.9 and F.R.10 were the last variants to be produced for the RAF, and there is no doubt that Hunter development was cut off too early, as indeed was production. This is partly because the type was regarded – mistakenly, as it turned out – as obsolescent in the late 1950s, partly because of the overly simplistic view of a future of push button missile warfare envisaged in the 1957 Defence White Paper, and partly because of the general loss of national self-confidence and political nerve that followed the Suez fiasco of 1956. Had development of the P.1083 with a thinner, more highly swept wing and reheated Avon, or a later truly supersonic version with a Rolls-Royce Spey turbofan and heavier attack loads, been allowed to continue, Britain would have had a type worthy to compete in the world fighter markets with the Northrop F–5 series and the F–104 Starfighter.

One interesting Hunter F.6 development projected was the P.1128 executive jet of 1957, which featured a cabin for six executive passengers seated side-by-side ahead of the wing with two pilots in front. The fuselage was similar to the F.6's but the Avon was replaced by a pair of Bristol Orpheus turbojets mounted side-by-side in the extreme rear fuselage under the fin and rudder, and fed by lateral air intakes aft of the trailing edge that replaced the wing root intakes.

Total Hunter production was 1,972, including Dutch and Belgian built ones, and here too many more Hunters – perhaps as many as 500 – could have been built and sold. As it was 302 Hunter fighters and 52 trainers were refurbished and updated for resale to more than a dozen air forces and 448 factory-new Hunters were exported (excluding Dutch and Belgian production), of which 50 were trainers.

Technical Description

Type: single-seat day fighter, ground-attack fighter, tactical reconnaissance fighter and ground-attack trainer, and two-seater trainer.
Wings: Cantilever all-metal stressed skin mid wing of 39° 54' sweepback at 25 per cent chord, and 8.5 per cent thickness/chord ratio. Hawker high speed symmetrical wing section. Anhedral 1°. Incidence 1° 30' at root. Extended 'dog tooth' leading edge extensions on Hunter F.6 and most later versions, applied retrospectively to many earlier mark Hunters. Ailerons powered hydraulically by Fairey Hydro-boosters. Electrically-operated trim tab in port aileron. Hydraulically-operated split flaps.
Fuselage: All-metal semi-monocoque stressed skin fuselage built in three sections: nose section containing cockpit, armament pack and nosewheel; centre section with integral wing root stubs, intake ducts and engine mounting attachments, and detachable rear fuselage with integral fin base and removable jet pipe and tail cone unit. Air brake hinged at forward end to underside of rear fuselage and extending through 67° of travel. Tail braking ring-slot parachute of 10-ft 6-in (3.20-m) diameter in fairing over jet pipe nozzle on FGA.9, F.R.10 and some exported Hunters. Hunter trainer variants seat instructor and pupil side-by-side in slightly wider forward fuselage that is 3 ft (1.02 m) longer than the single-seater FGA.9's, with fairing aft of cockpit canopy enlarged and recontoured according to area rule theory. Cockpit hood hinged to open upwards and backwards electrically.
Tail Unit: All-metal tail unit with sweepback on all surfaces; tailplane mounted on fin. 'Acorn' fairing at junction of rudder and elevators to prevent tail buffet at high subsonic indicated Mach numbers. Fully powered elevators with spring feel succeeded in 1957 on production Hunter F.6s by a 'flying tail' with the power-operated elevator interconnected to change the tailplane incidence electrically by Rotax actuator. Elevators actuated hydraulically by Fairey Hydro-boosters. 'Flying tail' operation of tailplane incidence through elevator can be cut out if desired by pilot-operated switch in cockpit. Electrically-operated trim tab in rudder.
Landing Gear: Retractable nosewheel type

The Royal Aircraft Establishment's Hunter T.12 XE531, converted from an F.6, was used extensively to test the Specto Avionics head-up instrument display intended for the BAC TSR.2.

undercarriage, with a single main wheel on each unit. Main wheels retract inwards into wing roots and nosewheel retracts forward; hydraulic actuation, with an emergency pneumatic system. Dowty liquid-spring shock absorbers. Dunlop wheels and tyres; Dunlop hydraulic wheel brakes with Maxaret anti-skid units. Main wheel tyre pressure of 200 lb/sq in (14.0 kg/cm^2) and nosewheel tyre pressure of 115 lb/sq in (8.10 kg/cm^2).

Power Plant and Fuel System: One 7,550 lb (3,423 kg) s.t. Rolls-Royce RA.21 Avon 113 in most Hunter F.1s and first 159 British-built F.4s; Avon 115 or 121 in later F.4s.
One 8,000-lb (3,629-kg) s.t. Armstrong Siddeley ASSa.6 Sapphire 101 turbojet in Hunter F.2 and F.5.
One 10,000-lb (4,540-kg) s.t. RA.28 Avon 203 in Hunter F.6 and T.66. Avons for Dutch- and Belgian-built F.4s and F.6s built under licence by Fabrique Nationale d'Armes de Guerre at Herstal in Belgium.
One 7,500-lb (3,400-kg) s.t. Avon 122 in Hunter T.7, T.8 and GA.11.
One 10,150-lb (4,604-kg) s.t. RA.28 Avon 207 in Hunter FGA.9, F.R.10, T.12, T.66B and T.67, also Hunters refurbished to Mk 9 standards.

Hunter FGA.9 has four flexible bag-type tanks in the fuselage and four in each wing. Front fuselage tanks of 200-Imp gals (909-litres) capacity and rear fuselage tankage is 52 Imp gals (236 litres). Total capacity of wing tanks 140 Imp gals (636 litres). Total fuel capacity 392 Imp gals (1,781 litres). Two or four 100-Imp gal (454-litres) asbestos phenolic drop tanks can be carried on underwing pylons, or two 230-Imp gal (1,045-litres) tanks on the inboard pylons. Hunter F.1 and F.2 had no provision for drop tanks; F.4 and F.5 could carry two 100-Imp gal (454-litres) drop tanks. Pressure refuelling through a coupling in the port main wheel bay.

Accommodation: Pressurised and air-conditioned cockpit with sliding jettisonable canopy. Pressure differential 3.5 lb/sq in (0.25 kg/cm^2). FGA.9 has increased oxygen reserves for pilot and boosted air conditioning for Middle East operations. Fully automatic Martin-Baker Mk 2H ejector seat, later fitted with the Duplex drogue system for safe ejections down to 125 ft (38.1 m). Mk 2H seats were later brought up to Mk 3H standard with higher ejection velocity. Hunter T.7, T.8 and export trainer variants seat instructor and pupil side-by-side with fully duplicated flying controls and gunsights; Martin-Baker Mk 4 fully automatic lightweight ejector seats. Hunter T.8Bs and T.8Cs have the TACAN navaid and OR.946 instrument display.

Armament: Four 30-mm Aden cannon with 150 rounds per gun in a self-contained removable pack in the underside of forward fuselage. Gun pack can be winched down for rearming and servicing. Automatic gun-ranging radar in tip of nose with scanner in nose radome,

and gyro gunsight. Hunter T.7 and T.8 had only one 30-mm Aden in the starboard side of the fuselage; this and radar ranging gunsight were removed from T.8B and T.8C to accommodate TACAN. Some Hunter trainers for export had two 30-mm Adens. Hunter GA.11 had cannon removed. The F.R.10 has one forward-facing and two oblique cameras in the nose; a camera nose has also been fitted to several Hunters refurbished for export to Mk 9 standards, and this nose can also be fitted to the GA.11.

The Hunter F.1 and F.2 had no provision for underwing 'stores', but the F.4 and F.5 could carry two 1,000-lb (454-kg) bombs or 100-Imp gal (454-litres) drop tanks on underwing pylons. Swedish Hunter F.50s were later modified to carry two Rb324 Sidewinder air-to-air infra-red homing missiles on the pylons. The Hunter F.6 and later variants had four underwing 'stores' pylons which could take on the inner pylons 1,000-lb (454-kg) or 500-lb (227-kg) bombs, or two small 25-lb (11.3-kg) practice bombs on a carrier; Hunter F.6s for export could carry four 400-kg or 200-kg bombs. BL–755 cluster bombs can also be carried.

A variety of rocket projectiles could be carried, typically three tiers of four No 1 Mk 5 3-in (76-mm) rockets with 12 lb (5.4 kg) warheads under each outer wing and two tiers of three rockets of the same kind on each inner pylon, all on the standard Mk 12 launcher rails. Rocket projectiles with a variety of warheads, of high explosive, armour-piercing or fragmentation kind, and weighing from 25 lb (11.3 kg) to 60 lb (27.2 kg) can be carried, and many different combinations of rockets and drop tanks are possible. Exported Hunter F.6s have been fitted with Oerlikon, Hispano, T.10 or Bofors rocket projectiles and rails, also HVAR and 'Tiny Tim' 5-in (127-mm) rockets. Two types of rocket pod, carrying 24 or 37 2-in (50.8-mm) spin-stabilised unguided folding fin rockets, can be carried, one on each inner pylon.

Some exported Hunter F.6s and Hunters refurbished to FGA.9 standard for foreign air forces were equipped to carry two AIM–9 Sidewinder air-to-air infra-red homing missiles, as were Royal Navy GA.11s. Swiss Air Force Hunter F.58s and F.58As are also fitted to carry the AGM–65 Maverick air-to-ground missile. Royal Navy Hunter T.8s and GA.11s were equipped to carry a Martin AGM–12B Bullpup–A air-to-surface missile under each wing.

Hunter Production

P.1067 Hunter prototypes: WB188 and WB195 with RA.7 Avon engines; WB202 with ASSa.6 Sapphire 101
Hunter F.1: 113 built at Kingston and 26 at Squires Gate
F.2: 45 built at Baginton by Armstrong Whitworth

F.3: WB188 converted from first prototype
F.4: 365 built in Britain, 188 at Kingston and 177 at Squires Gate. 108 built in Holland by Fokker and Aviolanda
F.5: 105 built at Baginton by Armstrong Whitworth
F.6: P.1099 XF833 was F.6 prototype; seven F.6 development aircraft (WW592-WW598). Total of 264 F.6s built by Hawker, and 119 by Armstrong Whitworth at Baginton. A further 237 F.6s were built or assembled in Holland and Belgium
T.7: Two prototypes, XJ615 and XJ627; 65 T.7s built at Kingston. Six F.4s converted to T.7s, and 31 more converted to T.8s for Royal Navy. A further 32 trainers were built for export as marks T.53, T.62, T.66, T.66B, T.67 and T.69, and 52 more trainers were refurbished for resale abroad, many of these being converted F.6s.
T.8: Prototype WW664 converted from F.4. Ten T.8s built at Kingston; 18 F.4s converted to T.8s, and 13 more F.4s converted to T.8Bs and T.8Cs.
T.8M: Three T.8s, XL580, XL602 and XL603, converted to T.8Ms with Sea Harrier's Blue Fox radar and avionics
FGA.9: 120 were converted from F.6s for the RAF. Twelve FGA.9s sold to the Rhodesian Air Force, five to Kenya and five to the Lebanon. A further 302 Hunter F.6s were refurbished and updated to basic FGA.9 standards for resale to foreign air forces, with mark numbers 70-78
F.R.10: 30 converted from F.6s; F.R.71A for Chile, F.R.74A for Singapore and F.R.76A for Abu Dhabi are very similar
GA.11: 40 converted from F.4s
T.12: One, XE531, converted from F.6 as test bed for Specto Avionics' head-up display for TSR.2
F.50: 120 delivered to Swedish Air Force (Flygvapnet) with the Swedish designation J34. Export variant of F.4
F.51: 30 delivered to Royal Danish Air Force. Export variant of F.4
F.52: 16 ex-RAF F.4s delivered to Fuerza Aérea del Peru
T.53: Two export variants of T.7 for Royal Danish Air Force
F.56: 160 for Indian Air Force, of which the first 12 were ex-RAF F.6s. A further 49 refurbished F.56As were acquired from 1966-67
F.57: 4 ex-Belgian F.6s refurbished for Kuwaiti Air Force
F.58: 100 for Swiss Air Force, of which the first 12 were ex-RAF F.6s. A further 52 refurbished F.58As were acquired from 1972-76
F.59: 44 for Iraqi Air Force refurbished from ex-Belgian F.6s
T.62: One export variant of T.7, serialled 681, for Fuerza Aérea del Peru
T.66: 22 trainers for Indian Air Force. A further 13 T.66Ds, converted from F.6s, were delivered from 1966-67. Also two T.66s to Lebanese Air force
T.66A: Hawker demonstrator G-APUX, rebuilt from damaged ex-Belgian F.6 with

forward fuselage of Indian Air Force T.66. Loaned to Iraqi Air Force with serial '567' during 1963-64, and then to Lebanon and Jordan. Sold to Fuerza Aérea de Chile in 1967 as J–718

T.66B: Three trainers for Royal Jordanian Air Force, two converted from ex-Dutch F.6s, this pair later being sold to Sultan of Oman's Air Force

T.67: Two trainers for Kuwait Air Force, plus three more refurbished from Dutch F.6s acquired later

T.68: Eight acquired for Swiss Air Force from 1972

T.69: Two for Iraqi Air Force, plus three more refurbished T.69s acquired later.

Refurbished Hunters updated to basic FGA.9 standard:

F.70: 17 to Lebanese Air Force

FGA.71: 30 to Fuerza Aérea de Chile from 1967, plus seven more ex-RAF FGA.9s supplied as Mk 71s in 1982

F.R.71A: Three to Fuerza Aérea de Chile

T.72: Four to Fuerza Aérea de Chile

FGA.73A and 73B: 32 to Royal Jordanian Air Force; all but one acquired in 1975 by Sultan of Oman's Air Force

FGA.74 and 74B: 34 to Singapore Air Defence Command, later renamed Republic of Singapore Air Force. Also four F.R.74As

T.75: Nine to Singapore Air Defence Command

FGA.76 and F.R.76A: Ten to Abu Dhabi Defence Force Air Wing from 1970. Later part of United Emirates Air Force, and disposed of in 1983 to the Somali Aeronautical Corps

T.77: Two to Abu Dhabi Defence Force Air Wing. To Somali Aeronautical Corps in 1983

FGA.78: Three to Qatar Emiri Air Force

T.79: One to Qatar Emiri Air Force

T.80: One to Kenya Air Force

RAF and RN Hunter Serials

P.1067 Hunter prototypes: WB188 and WB195 (RA.7 Avons); WB202 (Sapphire 101)

Hunter F.1: 113 Kingston-built: WT555-WT595, WT611-WT660 and WT679-WT700

Hunter F.2: 26 Squires Gate-built: WW599-WW610 and WW632-WW645 45 Baginton-built: WN888-WN921 and WN943-WN953 (WN905 crashed before delivery to RAF, and was not replaced)

Hunter F.3: WB188 converted from first prototype P.1067

Hunter F.4: 188 Kingston-built: WT701-WT723, WT734-WT780, WT795-WT811, VV253-VV281, VV314-VV334, VV363-VV412 and VV589-VV591

(11 converted to Hunter T.8, 20 converted to GA.11, VV272, VV318, VV383 converted to T.7)
177 Squires Gate-built: WW646-WW665, XE657-XE689, XE709-XE718, XF289-XF324, XF357-XF370, XF932-XF953, XF967-XF999 and XG341-2
(15 converted to T.8, 19 converted to GA.11, XF310 and XF321 converted to T.7)

Hunter F.5: 105 Baginton-built: WN954-WN992, WP101-WP150 and WP179-WP194

Hunter F.6: P.1099 prototype XF833; WW592-WW598 development a/c (WW593 and WW596 converted to F.R.10s)

Hunter F.6: 100 Kingston-built: XE526-XE561, XE579-XE628 and XE643-XE656 (30 converted to FGA.9 and 10 converted to F.R.10; six to Indian Air Force as F.56s, 12 to Swiss Air Force as F.58s)
91 Kingston-built: XG127-XG137, XG169-XG172, XG185-XG211, XG225-XG239, XG251-XG274 and XG289-XG298 (36 converted to FGA.9 and 2 converted to F.R.10)
45 Kingston-built: XJ632-XJ646, XJ673-XJ695 and XJ712-XJ718 (4 converted to F.6A, 26 converted to FGA.9 and 3 to F.R.10)
21 Kingston-built: XK136-XK156 (2 converted to F.6A, 8 to FGA.9)
100 Kingston-built cancelled in 1957: XK225-XK241, XK257-XK306 and XK323-XK355 (plus XK157-XK176 and XK213-XK224 completed for Indian Air Force as F.56s)
19 Baginton-built: XG150-XG168
100 Baginton-built: XF373-XF389, XF414-XF463 and XF495-XF527 (20 converted to FGA.9, 12 converted to F.R.10, six to Indian Air Force as F.56)
50 Squires Gate-built cancelled in 1957: XJ945-XJ959, XJ971-XJ997 and XK103-XK111

Hunter T.7: Two P.1101 prototypes XJ615 and XJ627
65 Kingston-built: XL563-XL579, XL583, XL586, XL587, XL591-XL597, XL600, XL601, XL605 and XL609-XL623 (plus XM117-XM126 diverted to Dutch Air Force as N–311 to N–320 and 10 more to Royal Navy as T.8s). Six F.4s converted to T.7s. Two ex-Jordanian and Saudi T.7s returned to RAF service as XX466 and XX467

Hunter T.8: First was WW 664, one of 31 converted from F.4s to T.8s, T.8Bs and T.8Cs. Ten T.8s built at Kingston: XL580-582, XL584, XL585, XL598, XL599 and XL602-604. XL580, XL602 and XL603 converted to T.8Ms

Hunter FGA.9: 120 converted from F.6s, the first being XE617

Hunter F.R.10: 30 converted from F.6s, the first being XF429.

Hunter GA.11: 40 converted from F.4s

Hunter T.12: One, XE531, converted from F.6

Preserved Hunters in the UK

Hunter F.1 WT612: (7496M) at RAF Credennig

Hunter F.1 WT680:Z (7533M) at RAF Aberporth

Hunter F.1 WT694:Y (7510M) 'gate guardian' at RAF Newton, Nottinghamshire

Hunter F.3 WB188: (7154M) at RAF St Athan Museum; previously with the RAF Colerne Museum and before that 'gate guardian' at RAF Melksham, Wiltshire

Hunter F.4 WT619: (7525M) at Manchester Air & Space Museum

Hunter F.5 7583M:E at RAF Henlow

Hunter F.5 WP185: at RAF Museum, Hendon

Hunter F.5 WP195:K 'gate guardian' at Stanbridge

Hunter F.6A XF509: (8708M) 'gate guardian' at RAF Chivenor

Hunter T.7 ET–273: ex-Royal Danish Air Force with The Bomber County Museum (formerly Humberside Aircraft Preservation Society) at Cleethorpes, Lincolnshire

Hunter T.7 G–BOOM: (ex-G–9–432, ex-ET–274 of the Royal Danish Air Force, and originally N–307 of the Dutch Air Force). Registered on 6 October 1980 to B.R. Kay at Leavesden, and later (29 September 1982) sold to Brencham Ltd at Hurn, a company formed by the owner of G–HUNT. Later (4 June 1984) to Brencham Historic Aircraft Co Ltd and now owned (since 5 October 1984) by Hunter Promotions Ltd of Hurn

Hunter F.51 E–407 ex-Royal Danish Air Force with the Leicester & Loughborough Aviation Museum & Preservation Society at East Midlands Airport

Hunter F.51 E–408:B ex-Danish is 'gate guardian' at RAF Brawdy

Hunter F.51 G–9–443: ex-E–412 of the Royal Danish Air Force with Tangmere Aviation Museum, West Sussex

Hunter F.51 G–HUNT: (ex-G–9–440, ex-E–418 of the Royal Danish Air Force). Bought by Spencer Flack from the makers in May 1978 and registered G–HUNT on 5 July that year for restoration at Elstree. First flew after restoration on 20 March 1980. Sold to M.R. Carlton on 2 October 1981; now owned (since 23 August 1984) by Brencham Historic Aircraft Co Ltd at Hurn.

Hunter F.51 E–419: (G–9–441) ex-Danish with The North East Aircraft Museum at Usworth, Sunderland

Hunter F.51 E–423: (G–9–444) with the Second World War Aircraft Preservation Society at Lasham, Hampshire. Used for spares during the restoration of G–HUNT

Hunter F.51 E–424: ex-Danish with the Lincolnshire Aviation Museum at Tattershall

Hunter F.51 E–425: ex-Danish with Midland Air Museum at Coventry/Baginton

Hunter F.51 E–427: ex-Danish kept at Hurn to provide spares for G–HUNT and G–BOOM

Hunter F.1

Type:	transonic day interceptor fighter
Accommodation:	pilot only
Armament:	four 30 mm Aden cannon with 150 rounds per gun in underside of forward fuselage. No provision for underwing 'stores'
Powerplant:	one 7,550 lb (3,423 kg) s.t. RA.21 Avon 113 turbojet

Performance:

maximum speed	693 mph (1,115 km/h) at sea level (Mach 0.9)
maximum speed:	617 mph (993 km/h) at 36,000 ft (10,973 m) (Mach 0.935)
typical cruising speed	—
initial climb rate	—
absolute ceiling	—
range	—

Weights:

empty	12,128 lb (5,501 kg)
normal loaded	16,200 lb (7,347 kg)
max overload	—

Dimensions:

span	33 ft 8 in (10.26 m)
length	45 ft 10½ in (13.98 m)
height	13 ft 2 in (4.26 m)
wing area (gross)	340 sq ft (31.5 m²)
aspect ratio	3.33

Hunter F.2

Type:	transonic day interceptor fighter
Accommodation:	pilot only
Armament:	four 30 mm Aden cannon with 150 rounds per gun in underside of forward fuselage. No provision for underwing 'stores'
Powerplant:	one 8,000 lb (3,629 kg) s.t. Armstrong Siddeley ASSa.6 Sapphire 101 turbojet

Performance:

maximum speed	698 mph (1,121 km/h) at sea level (Mach 0.905)
maximum speed	620 mph (997.8 km/h) at 36,000 ft (10,973 m) (Mach 0.94)
typical cruising speed	—
initial climb rate	—
absolute ceiling	—
range	—

Weights:

empty	—
normal loaded	—
max overload	—

Dimensions:

span	33 ft 8 in (10.26 m)
length	45 ft 10½ in (13.98 m)
height	13 ft 2 in (4.26 m)
wing area (gross)	340 sq ft (31.5 m)
aspect ratio	3.33

Acknowledgements

The author would particularly like to thank Mike Stroud of British Aerospace at Kingston for providing many of the black and white photographs for this book and also Ian Goold of *Flight International*. Grateful acknowledgements are also due to the following sources for illustrations:
Air Britain: pp. 13,49(top).
British Aerospace Kingston/Hawker Siddeley Aviation Ltd/Hawker Aircraft Ltd.: endpapers,pp.5,8,9,10/11,13,14,15(both),17, 18,20,22,24(top),26,27,28,31(both),42,43, 45(all),48,49(below),51(both),52.
Fairey Aviation Co Ltd.: pp.21(below).
Stuart Howe: pp.21(bottom).
Ministerie van Defensie Netherlands:pp.46.
Ministry of Defence: pp.1,16,19.
Rolls-Royce: pp.25(below).
Duncan Simpson: pp.47.

All colour photographs supplied by the author and Air Britain.

Hunter F.6

Type:	day interceptor and ground attack fighter
Accommodation:	pilot only
Armament:	four 30 mm Aden cannon with 150 rounds per gun in underside of forward fuselage. Four underwing 'stores' pylons – see Technical Description for details of 'stores' that can be carried
Powerplant:	one 10,000 lb (4,540 kg) s.t. RA.28 Avon 203 turbojet

Performance:

maximum speed	715 mph (1,151 km/h) at sea level (Mach 0.935)
maximum speed	627 mph (1,009 km/h) at 36,000 ft (10,973 m) (Mach 0.95)
typical cruising speed	515 mph (829 km/h)
initial climb rate	8,400 ft/min (2,560 m/min)
absolute ceiling	—
range	1,854 miles (2,987.5 km) with two 230 Imp gal and two 100 Imp gal drop tanks

Weights:

empty	13,270 lb (6,020 kg)
normal loaded	17,600 lb (7,983 kg)
max overload	24,000 lb (10,885 kg)

Dimensions:

span	33 ft 8 in (10.26 m)
length	45 ft 10½ in (13.98 m)
height	13 ft 2 in (4.26 m)
wing area (gross)	349 sq ft (32.43 m²)
aspect ratio	3.33

Hunter T.7

Type:	two-seat advanced trainer
Accommodation:	instructor and pupil seated side-by-side
Armament:	one 30 mm Aden cannon in starboard side of fuselage
Powerplant:	one 7,500 lb (3,400 kg) s.t. Avon 122 turbojet

Performance:

maximum speed	660 mph (1,062 km/h) at 20,000 ft (6,096 m) (Mach 0.935)
maximum speed	615 mph (990 km/h) at 40,000 ft (12,192 m) (Mach 0.93)
typical cruising speed	—
initial climb rate	10,500 ft/min (3,200 m/min)
absolute ceiling	49,500 ft (15,087.6 m)
range	—

Weights:

empty	13,360 lb (6,060 kg)
normal loaded	17,200 lb (7,802 kg)
max overload	22,500 lb (10,205 kg) (approx)

Dimensions:

span	33 ft 8 in (10.26 m)
length	48 ft 10½ in (14.90 m)
height	13 ft 2 in (4.26 m)
wing area (gross)	349 sq ft (32.43 m²)
aspect ratio	3.25

Hunter FGA.9

Type:	fighter and ground attack aircraft
Accommodation:	pilot only
Armament:	four 30 mm Aden cannon with 150 rounds per gun in underside of forward fuselage. Four underwing 'stores' pylons – see Technical Description for details of 'stores' that can be carried
Powerplant:	one 10,150 lb (4,604 kg) s.t. RA.28 Avon 207 turbojet

Performance:

maximum speed	715 mph (1,151 km/h) at sea level (Mach 0.935)
maximum speed	627 mph (1,009 km/h) at 36,000 ft (10,973 m) (Mach 0.95)
typical cruising speed	515 mph (829 km/h) at 30,000 ft (9,144 m)
initial climb rate	about 8,000 ft/min (2,440 m/min)
absolute ceiling	53,400 ft (15,911 m)
range	1,854 miles (2,987.5 km) with two 230 Imp gal and two 100 Imp gal drop tanks; 489 miles (787 km) with no drop tanks

Weights:

empty	14,400 lb (6,531 kg)
normal loaded	17,750 lb (8,051 kg)
max overload	24,000 lb (10,885 kg)

Dimensions:

span	33 ft 8 in (10.26 m)
length	45 ft 10½ in (13.98 m)
height	13 ft 2 in (4.26 m)
wing area (gross)	349 sq ft (32.43 m²)
aspect ratio	3.33

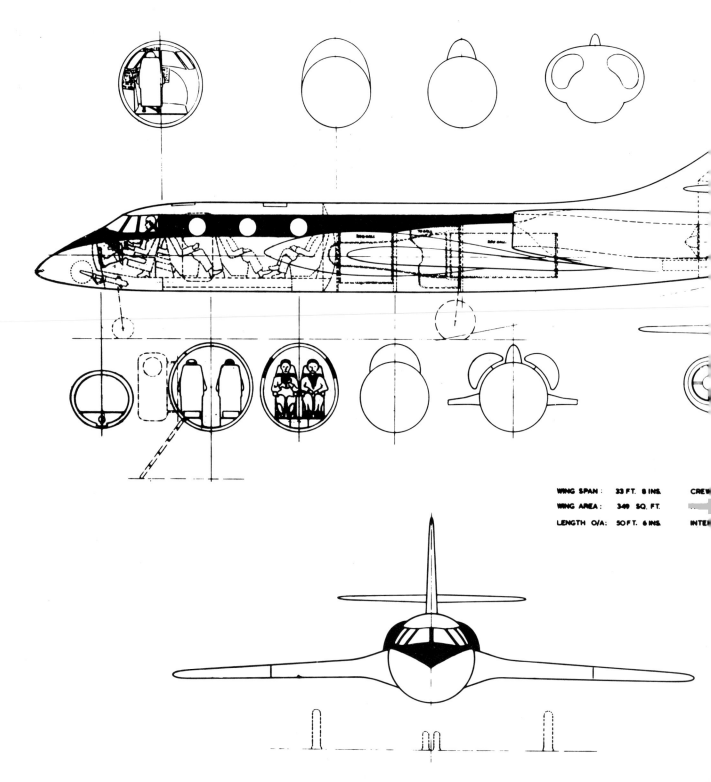

WING SPAN :   33 FT. 8 INS.   CREW

WING AREA :   340 SQ. FT.

LENGTH O/A: 50 FT. 6 INS.   INTER

HAWKE